Henry Baker Tristram

Rambles in Japan

The Land of the Rising Sun

Henry Baker Tristram

Rambles in Japan
The Land of the Rising Sun

ISBN/EAN: 9783337170745

Printed in Europe, USA, Canada, Australia, Japan

Cover: Foto ©Andreas Hilbeck / pixelio.de

More available books at **www.hansebooks.com**

PAGODA AND ENTRANCE TO LARGE TEMPLE, NIKKO.

THE LAND OF THE RISING SUN

BY

H. B. TRISTRAM, D.D., LL.D., F.R.S.

CANON OF DURHAM

WITH FORTY-FIVE ILLUSTRATIONS BY EDWARD WHYMPER

FROM SKETCHES AND PHOTOGRAPHS

AN INDEX AND A MAP

FLEMING H. REVELL COMPANY

NEW YORK   CHICAGO   TORONTO

The Religious Tract Society, London.

PREFACE

An apology may reasonably be expected for another book on Japan by one who has been a mere visitor, not a resident. The following pages are for the most part a transcript of the author's daily journal, written without any view to publication. But when, shortly after his visit, the eyes of the whole world were suddenly fixed upon the Land of the Rising Sun, and its unexpected display of military genius and power, it was suggested to him that his notes might be of interest, not only as describing some parts of the country seldom visited by foreigners, but as touching topics not generally dealt with by previous writers.

The primary object of the author's rambles was to master thoroughly the position of missionary work in Japan, especially that of the Church Missionary Society, and to ascertain the practical working of Buddhism as compared with the Buddhism of China and Ceylon. He had special advantages in being accompanied by his daughter, who, from her residence of some years in the country, her knowledge of the language and customs, and intense sympathy with the people, enabled him to gain an insight into many things which would otherwise escape the stranger's notice. He trusts also that his readers will forgive him, as a field naturalist, for many allusions to zoology and botany. He will be well rewarded, if he shall, however slightly, contribute to deepen interest in a race peerless among Orientals, and destined, when it has embraced that Christianity which is the only root of all true civilisation, to be the Britain of the Pacific.

CONTENTS

		PAGE
CHAP. I.	FIRST IMPRESSIONS	13
” II.	YOKOHAMA AND TOKIO	30
” III.	A VISIT TO NIKKO	81
” IV.	THE HAKONE LAKE	124
” V.	NAGOYA	164
” VI.	A SECOND VISIT TO KIOTO	195
” VII.	OSAKA	225
” VIII.	SHIKOKU	247
IX.	THE ISLAND OF KIUSHIU	266
” X.	ASO SAN AND THE GEYSERS OF YUNOTAN	286

LIST OF ILLUSTRATIONS

	PAGE
Pagoda and Entrance to Large Temple, Nikko	*Frontispiece*
Awazi Shima, on the Inland Sea	12
Nagasaki	17
Tsudzura Iwa Rock, Haruna	28
Arima	31
Vegetable Pedlar	37
Asakusa Temple, Tokio (Buddhist)	43
Zōjoji-zozo Temple	51
Japanese Soldier of the old time	56
Japanese Bronze Lantern	57
Ancient Japanese Archer	59
Japanese Buttons	61
Shiba Temple, at Tokio	67
Forest Trees near Nikko	80
Bridges near Nikko	85
Japanese Falconer	95
Stone Buddhas near Nikko	104
Lake of Chusenji	113
Buddhist Priest	117
Fujilama, from Omiya	125
Wayside Tea-house	131
Japanese Travelling Chair	140

LIST OF ILLUSTRATIONS

	PAGE
THE HAKONE LAKE, FIVE THOUSAND FEET ABOVE SEA-LEVEL	145
OJIGOKU, OR GREAT BOILING SPRING	150
PILGRIM GOING UP FUJIYAMA	158
NAGOYA CASTLE	167
TEMPLE AT NAGOYA, CONTAINING FIVE HUNDRED IMAGES	173
KISOGAWA RIVER	185
COLOSSAL IMAGE OF BUDDHA	194
TEMPLE AT KIOTO	199
A JAPANESE LADY	202
33,333 IMAGES, JAPAN	205
JAPANESE SHRINE SELLERS	209
WEAVING SILK	215
PLANTING OUT RICE	224
JAPANESE GIRLS, WRITING, SEWING, AND READING	231
A FLOWER-STAND IN THE STREET, OSAKA	244
LADY MISSIONARIES' HOUSE	249
THEATRE AT TOKUSHIMA	251
MISSIONARY'S HOUSE AT TOKUSHIMA	254
MISSION ROOM, TOKUSHIMA	255
COUNTRY BRIDGE	259
JAPANESE JUNK	264
KUMAMOTO CASTLE	282
COUNTRY PEOPLE CARRYING FIREWOOD	293

AWAZI SHIMA, ON THE INLAND SEA.

RAMBLES IN JAPAN

CHAPTER I

FIRST IMPRESSIONS

IMPRESSIONS are always heightened by contrast, and the first impressions of Japan, striking and enchanting as they must be in any case, were to me intensified by the startling contrast to the lands I had just left. As we stepped ashore in the lovely land-locked harbour of Nagasaki, and set foot on the little islet of Deshima, for two centuries and a half the only spot of Japanese ground which a European might tread, and those Europeans only half a dozen Dutchmen; and when one looked around on the harbour filled with shipping of every great nation in the world, and then on the sloping sides of the encircling rocky hills, dotted with fairy-like villas, peeping out amongst a labyrinth of semi-tropical trees, which overshadowed clumps of brilliant flowering shrubs, it was difficult to realise that only thirty-six hours before we had left the monotonous mud-banks and the turbid waters of the Yang-tsze-kiang. It was a veritable transformation scene.

The land of China, like its people, strikes one as essentially unromantic, everything on a large scale, dull and prosaic, matching the inhabitants, with many good qualities, solid, stolid, plodding, unimaginative—in short, a matter-of-fact, business land, nothing if not practical, but to a stranger's eye not much beyond. At once, after spending a day in the fogs of the Yellow Sea, we seemed to have stepped into fairyland; nothing grand, nothing magnificent, but everything in perfect harmony, a land of minute prettinesses. Well might my artist friend, who landed with me soon after sunrise, exclaim as we returned from our ramble through the streets: 'I should have come for six months instead of one, and brought a dozen sketch-books instead of two. Every step provides a new picture, every child in the street has an artist's eye. The little girls arrange their bouquets and sachets as though they were students of Ruskin; even the butchers' shops are decorated with vases and flowers, as though they were Regent Street repositories. Every woman looks bewitching, and the harmony of colours in a bright dress is a perfect study. Only one thing spoils the charm, the horrid intrusion of European slop tailors. While the porters and coolies attract one by their picturesque dress, fashion seems to demand from everyone who can afford it, that he should assume European hard hat, misfitting coat and trousers, and cotton gloves with elongated fingers. If the women are charming, the men look thorough little snobs.' I must endorse my friend's criticism, even though there be plain women in Japan as elsewhere.

Seaport towns, though generally the first

specimens that the traveller sees of a new country, are not necessarily the truest or most attractive representatives of their country. No exception can be taken to Nagasaki as an illustration of Southern Japan. For the capacity of its roadstead, it may well rank among the great harbours of the world. The entrance is somewhat intricate, but when once entered under the anchorage, we seemed to be in a land-locked lake surrounded by villas. Looking across the harbour, I was at once reminded of the Bay of Naples; I could have imagined myself gazing at Sorrento on a summer morning. But our minuter inspection soon revealed a difference: the general outlines might be similar, but there was a finish, an exquisite variety, an absence of whitewash and long stone walls, an adjusting and harmonising of every detail with its surroundings, which presented as fine an illustration of art concealing art as can be seen anywhere in the world. Every tree seemed placed as if it were a necessity where it grew, and where its absence must cause a disfiguring gap; the very shape of even the largest trees was guided by art which Japanese understand so well, for trees, like children, are there trained from their youth up: whilst the houses seem to suggest that they are a natural upgrowth from the rocks on which they stand.

Various little islets dot the inlet. I have mentioned the most historically celebrated, Deshima, the prison factory of the Dutch, where, since the expulsion of the Jesuits in the beginning of the seventeenth century, two Dutch ships a year were allowed to discharge and take in cargo, while the residents in the factory were never allowed to leave it. The islet is now united to the mainland by a causeway, and might be supposed by a stranger to be merely a continuation of the wharf. Near the farther end of the bay a lofty island cliff rises out of the water, the Tarpeian Rock of Japanese history, whence, according to the received tradition, many hundred native Christians, who refused to abjure their faith, were hurled into the depths beneath. The calm beauty of the scene to-day is indeed in strange contrast with its dark traditions.

Nagasaki, though one of the smallest cities of the first rank in Japan, yet from its situation and associations was selected as one of the treaty ports, open to Europeans, and is a most convenient trading port for the Southern Island of Kiushiu. It has not, however, increased in importance except as a mail station, the local trade being carried on at other ports. It has not a large European population, but it is the centre of the Church Missionary Society operations in the Southern Island, which has now at length a missionary bishop of its own. There is a rather handsome English church outside the city, and native churches within, as well as extensive schools.

The most important national establishment here is a medical college, the only one in the island, which bears very high reputation, and the professors in which are chiefly Europeans of scientific distinction. In fact, in nothing has Japan advanced more rapidly than in medical education, in which she is already in

NAGASAKI.

advance of some European countries. About thirty of the students at the time of my visit were Christians connected with the Church Missionary Society. They held a devotional meeting once a week in a native church for students alone, and had also one night for open discussion on Buddhism and Christianity, at which I happened to be present, and which was largely attended. The discussion was earnest and animated, though of course I could not understand a word.

It must be remembered that the island of Kiushiu presents many points of contrast to the other islands, both in climate, products, and character of the inhabitants. We are rather apt to forget the great variety there is in Japan on these points. With an area one-tenth larger than the British Isles, and the population larger in exactly the same proportion—forty-four millions to forty—the four main islands of Japan stretch slantways through sixteen degrees of latitude and twenty degrees of longitude. But, owing to its formation and number of islands, it possesses a coast-line more than double the extent of that of the British Isles. Like them, it enjoys the advantages of the warm equatorial current representing in the Pacific our own Gulf Stream.

In the variety of its natural products it vastly surpasses our own island group. In Yezo, the Northern Island, the hill-tops are the resort of the ptarmigan, identical with the bird of the Scottish Highlands; and the pine forests below are the home of the hazel hen, so familiar in the Swedish dahls. The great Central Island of Nippon (a name strangely corrupted into *Japan* by some of the earlier navigators) presents us with the varied produce of Northern and Central Europe, until in Kiushiu we have all the semi-tropical luxuriance of Andalusia and Southern Italy, and of even still more tropical climes. The traveller amongst the Ainu of the north may gather his bouquets of the lily of the valley and various Alpine acquaintances; whilst the wanderer amongst the villages of Satsuma in the south rests in the orange groves under the shade of the palm, lulled by the swish of the never-resting banana-leaves.[1] But as the British home possessions extend to the Shetlands northwards, and to the Channel Islands in the south, so the empire of Japan in the Kurile Islands possesses a continuation of insular territory to almost Arctic limits; while in the south the archipelago of the Loochoos, connected as they are with Kiushiu by an unbroken chain of islets, and beyond these again the Majico Sima group, close to Formosa, bring the island empire to the edge of the tropics, while the acquisition of the latter has brought it well within them.

The Japanese writers therefore may fairly claim that their empire stretches across the Temperate zone. Young Japan delights to talk of 'the Britain of the Pacific,' and considering the very good opinion these charming people had of themselves, even before the war of 1894, *we* ought to take this as a great compliment. And no doubt, with their vast seaboard, countless harbours, and inexhaustible sea fisheries,

---

[1] The banana lives, but does not bear fruit in Kiushiu.

they are a nation of born sailors, unapproached by any other Eastern nation. A Chinaman behaves well on the water so long as he has not to fight; a Japanese fisherman—and that is half the nation—is at home there. The fishing industry is perhaps quite as important to Japan as the raising of cereals; for, until recently, fish was the only animal food ever tasted by the people, and still is exclusively so except in European settlements. But I shall have much to say on this subject hereafter.

Long before the war with China, popular writers in Japan had set their heart upon the acquisition of Formosa, which can be easily understood on studying the map, and bearing in mind their maritime aspirations. In a book in my possession, written and printed in the English language at Tokio, the writer urges the importance of England securing Formosa at the earliest opportunity, as being the only security against the designs of Russia, who, the writer assumed, was prepared to absorb that island as well as Corea unless forestalled by England.

But it is not only in fisheries, it is also in mineral wealth, that Japan holds a position of pre-eminence which may be compared to that of Spain in Europe. The coal-fields, both in the south and north, are inexhaustible, and have scarcely been tapped. Even though very slightly developed, the yield of her copper-mines, after being worked for ages, far exceeds the demand, and there is reason to believe that the mineral deposits are equally rich in every department. Silver, it is said, used to be comparatively the scarcest of the metals, while gold was abundant, and stories are rife of the enormous fortunes made by American speculators at the first opening of Japan, between 1854 and 1868, who bought gold in the interior for twice its weight in silver. It would require, however, a very cute speculator to-day to make a profit out of a Japanese bullion dealer.

But enough of this preliminary digression. The detention of the steamer for coaling gave me the opportunity, which I did not miss, of visiting the outskirts of Nagasaki, as well as examining the beautiful manufacture of tortoiseshell articles, one of the staples of the place, and which in delicacy and minuteness of workmanship far surpasses the skill of Naples.

The coaling was carried on in very primitive fashion. The indigenous product (for the coal-mines are on an island at the other end of the bay, where they are worked by drifts run into the sides of the cliff) is passed from the barges in small baskets, head over head, by long lines of women and lads, chiefly the former, up the sides of the ship, and into the bunkers, while the empty mat baskets are passed back with equal rapidity by a parallel line of workers.

I was told that bunker coal at that time could be put on board for little more than a dollar a ton. Now, I believe, the price is very much higher, owing to the increased demand caused by the repeated strikes in England, and which have already led, throughout the whole of the Pacific ports, to the supplanting of Welsh and North of England coal by the cheaper and equally useful products of Japan, Vancouver Island, and even India. I have learned that since my visit the Japanese coal-mining (as might have been expected) has rapidly developed, and likewise the quality of the coal. Certainly, what we took in was very friable and dusty, but it was the product of an upper seam very near the surface, worked only by drifts in the side, while last year the lower seams, struck by sinking shafts, have yielded a superior quality.

I could not but notice the instinctive cleanliness even of the women who were working at coaling the ship. They had worn a sort of blue cotton poncho overall and a blue towel twisted on their heads, to protect their elaborately dressed hair from the dust. When they rested from work they at once threw off this outer cloak, carefully shook it, folded it into a small roll, and then, dusting their hair and washing their hands and face from the boat side, they shook themselves out and were as dapper and spruce as their neighbours.

As we walked on shore we were at once struck by the immense variety of flowering shrubs, all, at this season, one blaze of bloom, much less familiar to English eyes than those of the more northern parts, many of which are acclimatised at home; but few of those about Nagasaki can with us be more than greenhouse exotics.

The politeness even of boatmen and jinriksha men is overpowering, and the little wooden châlets which

line the roads, behind their dainty little flower-plots,
are indeed clean and bright.

As I afterwards travelled at leisure through a great
part of Kiushiu, I will say no more of this Devonshire or Kent of Japan. Our voyage next was to
Kobe, at the northern end of the famous Inland Sea.
Steamers to that port from China or the Strait
usually make it to the east of Shikoku, and so avoid
the circuitous and lengthy threading of the Inland
Sea, which, however, is, I believe, for beauty and love-
liness absolutely without a rival in the world. I do
not say this hastily, for I had the good fortune to
make the voyage three times—twice from south to
north, and once the return voyage; and these were
so timed that on one or other occasion I have traversed every mile of that fairy sea in full sunlight.
Let the traveller recall the finest bits of coast scenery
he can recollect — the Bay of Naples in spring,
Wemyss Bay on a summer's morning, a trip round
the Isle of Wight, threading the islands of Denmark's
Sounds, the luxuriance of the Sumatran coast, the
windings of the coral islets of Bermuda—recall which-
ever of them you please, wait but an hour or two—
and you will match it in the Inland Sea.

Before entering the sea itself, we were winding for
ten hours between the Archipelago of Goto and the
mainland northward, and then, turning eastwards,
crossed the Gulf of Genkai and steamed through
the narrow entrance into the Inland Sea, the
straits of Shimanoseki, *i.e.* Point of the Islands,
between the northern point of Kiushiu and the

farthest extremity of the main island Hondo, on which are the flourishing fishing and trading towns of Bakan on the north and Mōji on the south, the latter being prepared for a powerful battery of Armstrong guns.

The entrance to the sea is a narrow passage, apparently not more than two miles wide. It was a lovely morning as we entered. The whole scene baffles description : islands, bays, terrace-ribbed hills, woods of stately cryptomerias, wooden villages nestling in every recess—the distant ones, to use a very unpoetic simile, looking like clumps of mushrooms under the green ridges. The sea, resplendent as a mirror, was without a ripple, fleets of fishing junks were dotted about everywhere, sea birds, many species new to me in life, clumsily splashing out of our way, and diving about fearlessly on all sides. In these latter we were fortunate, for I saw comparatively few birds on subsequent visits. But the winter emigrants had not yet started for their summer homes. There were mergansers in great numbers, grebes of various species, and countless myriads of the Pacific species of puffins, shearwaters, guillemots and crested auks. There were also abundance of sea-ducks, scoters, scaups. It was simply a fairy scene which passes description. But alas! just at one of the finest points a dense fog abruptly met us, followed by a downpour of rain. The only thing was to anchor at once, till the fog should lift.

The scenery was equally enchanting during the whole of the rest of the voyage, but even beauty unvaried becomes monotonous, and we did not murmur at sunset robbing us of our scenery, nor rebel at the thought of retiring to our berths. Soon after dawn we could make our destination, the harbour of Kobe; very different from Nagasaki, comparatively more of an open roadstead, and a long straggling city, the most part of low wooden houses, with a few handsome terraces of stone houses, built European fashion, in front. Behind it on the south-east rises a range of hills about 1,000 feet high, on the lower slopes of which part of the town is built. A further range rising to 2,000 feet is the favourite summer resort of the inhabitants, known as Arima. To the northward extends a low, flat, uninteresting country of monotonous paddy-fields. We had to anchor far out, but European and Chinese harbour extortions do not appear to have reached Japan. We soon secured a little sampan, which tossed about very much like an empty tub, but landed us at the custom house for the moderate fare of $2\frac{1}{2}d.$ each. The customs examination was not rigorous, the officers being politeness itself, and though sorely puzzled by a tiger's skull and anteater's scaly covering, and amused by specimens of Chinamen's clothes, yet passed everything, even the prohibited Chinese embroidery, on my assuring them it was not for purposes of trade, but for presents to friends, and that I should buy far more in Japan. Then an officer observed to my daughter, who had come down from Osaka to join me here, 'Your father's friends will see how much better things there are in Japan than in China.'

TSUDZURA IWA ROCK, HARUNA.

The sketches which accompany this chapter, taken, as they are, from photographs, will explain much better than any description the varied character of the scenery of the Inland Sea. We may note the remarkable ingenuity with which pines of various kinds have been coaxed to grow on the top of every little isolated rock and out of the sides of every cliff. The pines being rooted in the cracks or crevices of the cliffs, are cleverly trained laterally to the desired length, and in the distance may be seen the solitary pine which, like a monument, crowns an isolated rock; while the fishing village nestled under the trees, with the boats drawn up in perfect security in the little cove which no storms can disturb, is a type of a thousand others which dot the shores of Japan. In some places somewhat lofty mountains approach the coast, especially on the east or Shikoku side; for a few hours after leaving the straits we pass the north-eastern point of Kiushiu, and are flanked on the eastward by the adjoining island of Shikoku, the fourth in importance of the Japanese group. The rocks of these mountains, chiefly igneous, often present very grotesque forms. It is difficult to imagine a more exact representation of a human bust than a rock in the forest of Haruna, as shown in the illustration.

CHAPTER II

YOKOHAMA AND TOKIO

Our steamer was to remain a day at Kobe, so we took the opportunity of spending the time at Osaka, the Manchester of Japan, only twenty miles from Kobe (accessible by frequent trains on a very European-looking railway).

For some little distance we ran along the foot of the hills, amongst which nestles out of sight Arima, the favourite summer resort, with its mineral springs and waterfalls. We soon, however, left the hills and crossed a monotonous plain intersected by a rectangular network of dykes and ditches, reminding one very much of the country between Haarlem and Amsterdam, and with cultivation yielding nothing in neatness and cleanliness to the Dutch.

Most of the compartments were paddy—that is, rice—fields. in a few of which the green blades were appearing above the black mud. But a very large number of the fields were cropped with rape just now in full bloom, one mass of golden yellow, and patches of cotton just budding, giving the whole plain the appearance of a chequered carpet spangled with yellow and green.

An hour brought us to Osaka, of which more anon.

ARIJA

But to the stranger who had just landed, the ways of the folk, their clean houses, lavish use of flowers, chubby clean children, with either dolls or babies strapped to their backs, pretty, bright women and girls, picturesque balconied houses, canals full of boats crossing the streets continually—all was novel and charming. But as I shall have occasion to write more of Osaka, and describe the missionary work, of which it is the centre, later on, I shall say no more at present.

We returned to Kobe, and re-embarked on board the magnificent Canadian-Pacific steamer Empress of India, Captain Marshall, R.N.R., and weighed anchor about midnight. Consequently we missed the coast scenery, and the next day, as it was blowing a gale of wind, we stood out to sea, and only had distant views of the mountain ranges. The following morning we landed at Yokohama.

This, the place where many travellers first touch Japan, the first treaty port, and the port of Tokio, the capital, owes its importance entirely to foreign trade. It was merely a fishing village in 1854, but now a magnificent esplanade of splendid houses in the European style faces the sea, not at all Japanese in their character. On both sides a straggling native town of mean wooden shanties extends along the shore; whilst behind, a bold eminence, known as the Bluff, within the limits of the foreign concession, is covered with handsome villas, gardens, and winding drives. For the stranger who wishes to see the Japan of the Japanese, Yokohama can have but few attractions; the miscellaneous crowd drawn to a great seaport being by no means improved by contact with foreigners, but too often imitating the vices they see, and losing their native simplicity. At the same time the emporiums on and near the esplanade contain by far the finest assortment of Japanese wares and curios, at the best prices, to be found in the empire.

Amidst much in the port that is distressing to a Christian Englishman to hear of and witness, I must not omit to mention a specially bright spot, the Sailors' Home, combined with the missions to seamen afloat, under the direction of the admirable chaplain, the Rev. W. T. Austin, and his indefatigable wife Dormitories, dining-room, and recreation-room are all well furnished, whilst an attractive reading-room is more liberally supplied with papers, magazines, and light reading than one often finds out of England; many of the merchants and agents who are indifferent about evangelistic efforts being very willing to contribute to this branch of the work. It was pleasing to see how many American and English sailors appreciated the place. I had not an opportunity of seeing the work of the American missionaries in the native town, of which I heard good reports.

As an illustration of American enterprise, the first letter that was handed to me before I left the ship was one from a dealer in birdskins, who had seen my name in the passenger list, and, recognising me as a naturalist, sent a special invitation on board by his agent. I must confess he was rewarded for his pains.

In order to see the city we embarked in jinrikshas, the universal hansom cabs of Japan. They are, in fact, a light armchair with a hood, on a pair of bicycle wheels, with long shafts, and a coolie running between them. It was long before I could reconcile myself to the sensation of being dragged about by a brother man, but it is really the only mode of locomotion, except one's own legs, possible in this country outside the railways, and as a Japanese once said to me, ' Why should you object to a man-drawn carriage ' (literal translation of jinriksha), ' when you have no objection to being pulled by a man in a boat ? '

Towards evening we went by rail to Tokio. The railway system is much on the American plan, with the important exception that there are always three classes of carriages; but most are long and open down the centre, and well ventilated. The country through which we passed was rich and thoroughly cultivated. On one side, the Bay of Tokio studded with shipping, a rice-covered plain intervening. On the other, a range of low hills with picturesque brown wooden cottages, frequent little temples and shrines marked by the Shinto gateway, one of the universal features of Japan ; and orchards of fruit-trees. On one part of the plain was an expanse of pear-trees, all trained on trellises like the vines of Italy, and in full bloom ; the peach and cherry were everywhere in the glory of full blossom. In fact, it is chiefly for the blossom that these fruit-trees are cultivated. The plums are little better than sloes, the cherries very small, and the peaches poor. So little are the fruits appreciated that there are more double-blossoming than single-blossoming trees, and the blossom by cultivation has been developed to three times the size of the corresponding bloom at home—the cherry bloom often attaining the size of our wild rose, and the peach that of a double daisy. There was nothing grand on the route, but everything attractive, neat, clean, and sweet, perfectly in keeping with the bright little folk who cover the land. We found ourselves the only foreigners in the long American car, and whilst my daughter talked to some girls, a young Japanese came and sat by me, and tried to air his English, which was very scanty, and which at first I did not recognise, but which pleased him mightily. From the station we rode in jinrikshas through wide streets with the most picturesque-roofed, one-storeyed houses, and open shops decked in the gayest colours. All was wood, paint, and paper. It was really like living on a Japanese screen. Canals almost as numerous as streets; and by the side of all this old-world quaintness, tramways and 'buses, telegraph poles—one of which carried sixty-four wires as I counted them—and here and there the whistle of engines, and the chimneys of factories; now and then little boulevards with rows of peach-trees, one blaze of bloom.

Tokio—that is the east capital—was known as Yedo until 1868, when the Mikado took up his residence there instead of at Kioto or Saikio, the west capital. It is a vast place extending many miles, and having a population of one million three

VEGETABLE PEDLAR.

hundred and eighty-nine thousand souls, but very flat, the greater part of its area having been recovered from the sea within the last three centuries; the favourite quarter of Shiba on a low ridge being the Highgate and Hampstead of the place.

We were quartered for a few days at Tsukiji, in the European concession, with a hospitable friend, the Rev. J. Williams, of the Church Missionary Society. Missionaries in Japan have a great advantage in that the people are not jealous of *Christian*, but rather of *foreign*, influences, and keenly appreciate the value of education. The educational system in Japan, whether elementary, secondary, or higher, is very complete and perfectly organised. The government subsidises it liberally, and Christians are perfectly untrammelled, while there are Christian professors in the University, and Christian masters in the schools. The empress, who takes a lively interest in education, has established a college for ladies with handsome buildings, where the daughters of the nobility resort.

The strange juxtaposition of East and West, of indigenous and European civilisation, never ceases to impress one: all the women in native bright costume, many of the men in European dress more or less well fitting. But still the native costume predominates in Tokio. Everyone carries his insignia embroidered on the back of his blouse or coat: *employés* have the name of the firm in huge hieroglyphics or Chinese characters covering the whole of their back; gentlemen always have their crest embroidered about the size of a dollar between their shoulders. The huge hieroglyphics on the backs of the labouring men are supposed to be the distortions of ancient Chinese characters, though even the learned are now unable to decipher them. The armorial bearings of the gentry are rigidly hereditary. The Japanese have a very ancient and highly systematised heraldry, quite distinct in its idea from our bearings and shields, and taken chiefly from leaves and flowers. Thus the ordinary imperial crest, as emblazoned on all the Mikado's carriages, is the chrysanthemum; and another, the more official, crest is the blossom of the paulonia, consisting of three upright spikes of blossom, like that of the horse-chestnut, in a row, with three leaves hanging down below. The insignia of the latest Shogun dynasty was a trefoil taken from a large species of the herb Paris. The Shoguns, or mayors of the palace, were commonly known to Europeans before the opening of Japan as Tycoons, a corruption of the Chinese Tai Kwon, *i.e.* great general. These crests or badges are impressed on all the old porcelain and bronze, and indicate at once in what district or under what Daimio the article was manufactured.

The palace of the emperor, with its widely extended parks and moats, occupies the site of the old castle and grounds of the Shoguns. The park is surrounded by a wide and deep moat, the enclosing walls of which are of enormous cyclopean masonry. In places it is almost choked with lotus and several species of water lily, and crowded with wild duck, amongst which the beautiful mandarin duck is most conspicuous. Within the moat are the old magnificent walls, absolutely impregnable before the days of gunpowder. Passing over a drawbridge and through the gateway, we enter the outer radius, laid out as a beautifully kept park. Within this are a second moat and encircling walls, quite as wide and massive as the outer circuit. Within these again are the private grounds, gardens, and palace of the emperor. I should have mentioned that in the outer park, after crossing the first moat on the right, was the *débris* of an extensive range of wooden buildings which had lately been destroyed by fire, and which, with the usual promptness of Japan, crowds of workmen were busily employed in clearing away: already they had commenced their reconstruction. These ruins were those of the first Parliament-house of Japan, which, having closely imitated the English Constitution in its two houses of Legislature, of which the upper is partly hereditary and partly nominated for life, further imitated us in the burning down of its first St. Stephen's, though after a much shorter experience. We can only trust that the carefully devised institutions of Japan may be more permanent than their first home.

Beyond the site of the Parliament-houses is a wide parade ground, answering to our St. James's Park. On the other side of the park is a vast range of buildings, the offices of the various government departments, in which our own subdivisions of the Treasury, Home Office, Education, etc., etc., have been pretty closely followed. Here also is the government printing office, and the manufactory of bank-note paper, which is a legal currency. Strangers are permitted to see the printing office.

The palace itself was not open to visitors when we were there, as it was occupied by the emperor. In its outline it follows the antique Japanese architecture, while a great part of it is internally furnished after the European fashion.

Just beyond the outer moat of the imperial park is situated the British legation. I cannot sufficiently acknowledge the courtesy and kindness of our minister, the late Mr. Frazer, whose recent death we have to deplore; through whose kind efforts we at once obtained special passports enabling us for six months to travel wherever we pleased, without being troubled by the police authorities, a favour which is very rarely granted, and which caused us to be the envy of many of our compatriots. I had letters to Count Ito, and recommendations from the Foreign Office as a scientific man much interested in educational work. These proved of great value in my rambles.

Our next day's sight-seeing was an expedition to Uyeno, the Hyde Park or South Kensington of Tokio. Here have been held three national industrial exhibitions. Of course, as we had a journey of some miles across the city, we made the expedition in jinrikshas, or, as they are commonly called by the Japanese, kurumas. I now experienced for the first, but not the last, time the tantalising inconvenience of this Japanese mode of travelling. There were four of us

in a line, quite unable to converse, while I, seeing every minute new and perplexing sights, with my daughter just in front of me, but quite unable to ask her a question, was obliged to be content with the contemplation of the back of her hat. The speed which our coolies keep up is really amazing. They maintain the rate of five miles an hour, and frequently a greater speed if the distance be short. On one occasion two men with one kuruma kept up this speed for four hours without a moment's halt. At length, as we approached Uyeno, we came to a slight ascent, and were very glad to get out and walk, though one frequently finds that the men consider the attempt to walk uphill a slight upon their powers, and try to prevent one from alighting. Entering the park, we visited the Technical Museum, that of Natural History, and that of Japanese Antiquities.

The Natural History Museum is only in its infancy, and the industrial department gives a very good illustration of the various manufactures, textile, metal, porcelain and lacquer, of the country. But the national antiquities are such as can be seen and studied nowhere else. They begin by the stone arrow-heads, spear-heads, celts, and pottery of the prehistoric period, differing very slightly from our own. Some of the rude pierced ornaments and beads are still in use in the Loochoo Islands, and of exactly the same shape, thus giving us one of the very few indications we possess as to the origin of the early inhabitants of Japan. Next follow, as in Western Europe, the mirrors, utensils, and weapons of the bronze period, with pottery of a less rude character. Then follow a large collection of various articles, and of pottery figures of men, horses, and birds, which were found in great quantities inside the funereal mound of one of the earlier emperors. The next hall is devoted to antiquities of the historic period, the earliest certain date being A.D. 708, from which period downwards there is a fine collection of coins; the ancient coins were not circular, but oblong, some of the gold ones very large and covered with hieroglyphics, but no busts. The other antiquities are chiefly of Buddhist origin; but one of the most interesting collections is that of the Christian relics, especially those brought by the embassy sent to Rome by the Prince of Sendai, A.D. 1614.

There is an amusing difference in the Japanese and Roman versions of this embassy. The European writers state that the envoy went on the part of the Shogun to recognise the supremacy of the pope, who in return presented him with the freedom of the city of Rome and loaded him with presents. The Japanese, on the contrary, state that the Shogun sent the envoy in order to report upon the political power and military strength of the European nations. Amongst the relics is a Latin deed conferring on Hashikura the freedom of the city of Rome, a picture of him in prayer before the crucifix in his European costume, and copies of the prince's letters to the pope in Japanese and Latin. By the side of these are shown the trampling boards—*i.e.* large metal slabs, with figures of the Virgin and Child, and of the different incidents of the Passion — on which suspected Christians were compelled to trample in order to testify their abjuration of Christianity. This collection must be one of the most touching interest to every Christian.

In other halls are exhibited the quaint furniture and trappings used by the Mikado and Shogun and their courts up to the time of the present generation. The most curious are an ancient bullock carriage and palanquins, most richly carved and gilded, as well as the state barge used by the Shoguns. These bullock carriages bear the same relation to the kuruma of to-day that the state coach of Queen Elizabeth does to a modern landau. There was also the throne of the ancient Mikados, with the rich silk hangings that used to conceal him from the gaze of his subjects, who were only allowed to see his feet. Some of the state carriages are three hundred years old, and the lacquer work and porcelain jars are of untold value. There is, besides, a fine collection of old Japanese armour and swords.

We went next to the Zoological Gardens, which are only in their infancy. Two sheep in a cage between some small bears on the one side and leopards on the other were evidently the most popular curiosity. They were taken for lions, and when they bleated some of the children exclaimed, 'Lions roaring!'

We then went on to a very fine Shinto temple, the arrangement consisting of various separate buildings.

Facing the shrine of the central temple was a large hall, quite open in front; in fact, the stage of a theatre, with roof and walls of wood most gorgeously carved, gilded and painted. A play was being performed. All the actors were men dressed in antique costume; all wore masks, some of them grotesque, and there was much pantomime and recitation. The theatricals seemed to resemble what I had seen in Chinese temples, and, evidently connected more or less directly with the worship, reminded me of what one reads of the miracle plays of the Middle Ages.

We turned round—the temple shrine was just in front of us, much like another stage, almost the counterpart of the theatre. Within the shrine was only a large circular disc or mirror of burnished metal, with long strips of white paper suspended from inscribed tablets on either side. In front of it a lavish display of lights burning; a number of priests in green vestments with strange instruments, all sitting on the elevated platform and producing weird music; below this dais the people kneeling in prayer, frequently clapping their hands; while the whole sacrarium was covered with small coins, called rin, the value of each being the twentieth of a penny, which the people threw, aiming them at a large box placed in the middle of the sanctuary. This we found was a great function—the anniversary of the death of one of the Shoguns.

The Shinto worship is utterly different from the Taouism of China, and has none of its gross idolatry. In some respects it is analogous to the old Persian fire worship, the mirror representing the sun, who himself is the representative of the invisible Deity, while the Mikado is the human representative of the sun, and therefore, in some degree, a partaker of the divine nature. Nor is this all the meaning of the mirror, the great feature of Shinto worship. In it man is supposed to see his own heart mirrored, and, comparing it with the purity of the white paper by its side, to see wherein he fails, and correct it. A Japanese was supposed to be superior to any moral code; one glance at his heart was sufficient, and he would certainly reform himself.

Close by are the tombs of the Shoguns, with two mortuary temples. The carving and gilding of these temples is lavishly rich in barbaric splendour. The whole structure is exclusively of wood, the ground colour of everything being painted red, upon which the most skilful native art has been lavishly employed both in painting and sculpture. Their open-work carving of birds and flowers, the symbolic chrysanthemum predominating, is mingled with the richest arabesques; the columns are wreathed with plum-blossoms in red and gold, the beams with lions' heads also in red and gold. Within the shrines are memorial tablets, sumptuous specimens of the most costly gold lacquer, commemorating the dead. Another temple contains the shrines of the mothers of eight Shoguns. Amongst the fantastic animals which decorate the panels of these buildings I was surprised to notice both the unicorn and the phœnix, probably suggested in the sixteenth century by the intercourse of Japan with Western Europe. An even finer temple than these formerly existed on the site of the museum, but was burnt down five-and-twenty years ago, during a battle fought in this park between the troops of the Mikado and those of the last Shogun.

Passing from the temples, we walked under a gorgeous avenue of cherry-trees, just now in full blossom and at this time the great attraction of Tokio. It is difficult to describe the exquisite beauty of the pink cherry-blossom. It is like nothing else, and has been called 'uniquely beautiful.' One looks up and the air seems filled with pink clouds. The natives, with their instinctive eye for beauty, are never tired of these promenades. On one occasion, when we were making an excursion, our kuruma men begged to be allowed to take us round by the cherry avenue. When we replied that it would be more than a mile out of our way, the men said they would charge us nothing more if we would only go, for the beauty of the place would abundantly reward them. I have not met with a London cabman with such an appreciation of the beauty of our parks in spring. One of the striking features of the Uyeno temples are the colossal bronze standard lanterns, some of them eight or ten feet high, which are placed singly or in rows leading up to the temple. Immense stone lanterns of the same model often occur in various temple grounds. It is difficult to estimate the enormous value of the metal of the solid bronze masses. They are the gift of various great Daimios or other rich

ZŌJOJI-ZOZO TEMPLE. STONE LAMPS GIVEN BY DAIMIOS IN HONOUR OF THE VARIOUS SHOGUNS BURIED THE NAMES OF DONORS ARE ENGRAVED ON THE STEMS OF THE LAMPS.

men to the memory of the Shoguns, and each lantern has the name of the donor inscribed upon it.

After these reminiscences of the Japan of the past, I spent two days in visiting the University of Tokio, the embryo Japan of the future. The Imperial University is intended for the whole country, and is the only university in the empire. All students must have previously passed through one of the three great colleges, which are supported by the government, and of which there is one in the island of Kiushiu and two in Hondo. There are more than 1,300 students at the university. I met a number of professors, most of them native gentlemen, graduates of Cambridge, Leipsic, and Harvard, amongst them a wrangler and two English professors, both Fellows of the Royal Society. I had an introduction to Dr. Ijima, the head of the zoological department, where there is really a fine national collection, and the nucleus of a good general museum. I was invited to dine in the common-room with the professors, who all spoke English fluently. The dinner, however, was not purely Japanese, for knives and forks and European as well as native dishes were generally patronised. The students do not reside in college, nor is there any collegiate discipline. They appeared generally to wear a dress modified from our cap and gown.

I was much interested with the botanic gardens, and learned a good deal from the curator, as well as from the gardeners who happened to be employed by my host, of the Japanese arts of dwarfing, transplanting, and distorting trees and shrubs. They successfully transplant forest trees at any age. They have dwarf pines, cryptomerias, maples, and oranges, living and healthy, only a few inches high, with leaves blossom, fruit, all equally liliputian, in perfect proportion. They are extremely fond of the grotesque and artificial How the double blossoms and the spotted foliage plants, of which they are so fond, are produced, I was not able to ascertain. Most effective are the trees, maples and others, in which the foliage of each branch is of a different colour. Thus I have seen a well-grown maple-tree with seven large limbs, each having foliage of a different hue, varying from dark copper to pink and greenish-white—this, of course, by grafting. The trees that are intended to be dwarfed are placed in pots alongside of a wire frame; it may be two or three feet in height, or perhaps only a few inches. This frame represents the exact number, shape, and size of the branches the tree is to be allowed to have; and every branch is bound to the wire or else cut off. The roots are carefully pruned and confined, and the young foliage is unceasingly nipped off. The transplanting of full-grown trees was very simple. The roots were simply laid bare, taking especial care to preserve the most delicate fibres, and, as soon as the earth has been cleared away by the fingers or sticks, not with spades, lest they should be bruised, each bunch of rootlets is confined in a little cotton bag. I have seen a tree moved in this way which required twenty men to move it with rollers. When the tree is placed in its new position, the bags are unloosed one by one,

JAPANESE SOLDIER OF THE OLD TIME.

and fine, pulverised soil carefully sprinkled between the fibres, no rootlet being allowed to touch another. They attach great importance to the work of transplanting, which is always begun in the evening, being completed before the heat of the next day. However, Japanese gardening is an art which it evidently requires years to master, and which would well repay the student of plant life.

Charming as are the buildings and scenery of Uyeno, they are certainly in almost every point excelled by those of Shiba, situated at the southern end, as Uyeno is at the northern, of the great city. We spent portions of several days in visiting this maze of gardens, temples, and tombs. The great street leading to it contains the most interesting shops of every kind, the type of which is but little spoiled by European innovations. Here is the Wardour Street of Tokio.

JAPANESE BRONZE LANTERN.

I was most attracted by the fine collections of the ancient armour, now—alas, for picturesque quaintness!—utterly discarded. As one watched the nimble battalions of little riflemen marching through the streets on their way to or from parade in their Frenchified uniform, and now read of their prowess against their hereditary rivals, we could hardly realise that not only the grandfathers but the fathers of these dapper little men had paraded these same streets in all the glory of their mediæval accoutrements, weighted with chain armour and steel helmets, and girt with their two swords.

The collections of old armour and swords in these shops were to me as fascinating as a display of the fashions in Regent Street to an English belle, while the prices, as far as I could judge, were extremely moderate. I made many purchases at a price really less than the value of the material. Amongst the most beautiful specimens of Japanese art were the richly inlaid guards of the swords, elaborately worked in gold or silver in endless artistic devices. Some of the sheaths also were exquisitely ornamented in the same fashion. In fact, ancient armour was at this time a drug in the market, many of the poorer Samurai being compelled to part with their treasured accoutrements for rice. We purchased several swords of very fine temper for moderate prices, but the work of some of the celebrated artificers of these blades still commands a fancy price, their reputation surpassing the reputation of the finest Damascus blades. The names of some few of these artificers are handed down for many generations, and their blades, which are marked and recognised, are treasured as a Stradivarius would be by a musical connoisseur.

There were also for sale large collections of nitsuki, or ivory carvings—a kind of large button used for

ANCIENT JAPANESE ARCHER.

fastening the inevitable pipe and pouch into the girdle. Some of these are exquisitely carved, and are masterpieces of art — mice nearly life size, squirrels and various small animals in all sorts

JAPANESE BUTTONS.

of attitudes, where the artist has indulged his lively fancy in every form of grotesque humour. These sculptured nitsuki are pierced with two holes, through which a silk cord is passed, on which used to be hung little bags of flint and steel, tobacco and bamboo pipe with its tiny brass bowl. The flint, steel, and tinder-box are of course now superseded by matches. The grotesque generally preponderates in these nitsuki, but many of them are historical figures or illustrations of domestic life. In fact, from these carvings one may get as complete an idea of Japanese life as we may of Egyptian from the frescoes by the Nile. Ivory has evidently been a most abundant material in Japan until recently, but it is not the ivory of the elephant from India. It is said to have been imported from Corea, whither it had been brought from the shores of the Arctic Ocean, strewn with the tusks of the prehistoric mammoth.

Being in search of a butterfly-net, or the wherewithal to make it, I was directed to the shop of a dealer in fishing-tackle. It was interesting to find that the trout and salmon of Japan succumb to the same wiles as their fellows in Northern Europe. But while the flies were home-made, the hooks themselves were all supplied from Redditch, the wares of which have completely supplanted the native manufacture. Gaudy salmon flies, brown palmers, and other familiar types, recalled, in that far-off land, the memories of many a Northumbrian 'burn.' We found, too, a taxidermist's shop; for the study of Nature in all its branches, botany especially, was appreciated by the Japanese long before the country was opened to intercourse with Europe. While rummaging his stores, I came across an excessively rare bird from the Loochoo Islands, of which only two or three specimens had ever reached Europe. I had found his prices very moderate, but for this he asked me five dollars. I demurred to the price, but I have always found the Japanese are at once fetched by a joke; and so, when he told me that the dealer in live birds across the street asked twenty-five dollars for a living bird, I replied, through my daughter, that such a good man as he was worth a thousand dollars when alive, but I would be sorry to give ten for him when dead. The dealer threw himself back, laughing heartily at the joke, and said I might have it for a dollar.

But nothing in this street was more interesting to me than the shops of the dealers in live birds. I have never been able to ascertain how the Japanese succeed in keeping in captivity many species which with us pine and perish in confinement. One of the commonest cage-birds is the titmouse, all the species of which, several of them identical with, or closely allied to, our own, as the great, marsh, and cole-tits, seem most happy and healthy in their little bamboo prisons. The Japanese robin, a close cousin of our own, and only to be distinguished by his under-parts being steel-grey where ours are white, is also a very favourite cage-bird. I often thought, when I saw robins, titmice, warblers, and the like, singing brightly and evidently at their ease in their cages—birds which we never, or very rarely, succeed in domesticating—that there must be something very sympathetic in the Japanese nature, some magnetic attraction between them and the birds, which is foreign to our more phlegmatic Western nature. I was struck, too, by the contrast, in appearance and plumage, between the sprightly cage-birds of Japan and the draggled, miserable-looking captives which I have seen in the Chinese bazaars. But the Japanese cultivates his captives because he loves them; the Chinaman entraps them to trade with the foreigner. The abundance of swallows skimming in all the streets, and threading their rapid flight between the heads of the passers-by, must strike the most unobservant. Scarcely a house or shop in Tokio is without one pair at least of these cheery little summer residents. They are of two species, one scarcely to be distinguished from our own chimney swallow, the other the red-rumped swallow, almost as abundant, but easily to be distinguished by the bright red of the lower back, and its streaked throat and breast. There being no chimneys, both species adapt themselves to circumstances and build on the rafters and ledges of the houses and shops, within reach of any passer-by, flitting in and out with the fearlessness of domestic pets. To molest them would be a crime equal to rudeness to a fellow-creature. And in order to prevent any dirt or untidiness, a thin board is carefully suspended under every nest, and daily cleaned. Our chimney swallow finds a ledge to build his open nest, but the other attaches his mud structure to the roof, after the fashion of our window martin, and for greater security adds a funnel-shaped passage about a foot long of the same material. Hence they are called in the country 'the bottle swallows.'

But we have lingered long on the way to Shiba! Shiba has a charm of its own in the fact of its being on rising ground; and the magnificent and noble trees certainly are an exception to the ordinary diminutiveness of most things in Japan. As a friend remarked when he had first seen an avenue of gigantic cryptomerias, 'It is worth coming to Japan to see the cryptomeria at home.' The floral glories of the islands were at their height. The glowing sheets of colour covered the double-blossoming cherries and peaches of every hue, from the deepest crimson to the purest white, in great masses; and then the cryptomerias, maples, Salisburias, and other trees, with their pale and dark foliage, were grouped artistically in a way of which we have no conception.

But the central attractions of Shiba are the shrines sacred to the memory of Shoguns of the Tokugawa family, six of whom are buried at Uyeno, two at Nikko, and six at Shiba, whilst the last deposed prince is still living. These shrines are of very rich woodwork, with the most elaborate gilding, approached through numerous groups of colossal stone lanterns. We enter by a gateway whose pillars have metal dragons twisted round them, and are gilt. The court inside this gate is lined with two hundred and twelve huge bronze lanterns, the gift of different Daimios during the last two centuries. Through a third gate are galleries with richly painted panels and carved birds and flowers, while the beams of the roof of the temple are carved into the shapes of dragons. Here we had to take off our shoes before we entered what may be called the chancel or sanctuary. Within the inmost sanctuary are shrines in which are concealed

F

the statues of the different Shoguns. But these images, the gifts of emperors, are never shown, so that there are no images visible. On the outer platform the Samurai and lesser gentry used to worship, whilst in the corridor leading to the inner sanctum the great Daimios were admitted ; the Great Shogun alone worshipping in the inner sanctuary. On either side of the shrines are wooden statues of the guardian angels, who are supposed to protect the world against demons. The outer courts of these shrines are decorated with barbaric magnificence. The most gorgeous gold lacquer is held together by costly and beautifully executed metal work. It is curious to note amongst the favourite decorations the unicorn, the fabled animal, which seems to be recognised in the East as well as in the West. Behind these gorgeous temples a long flight of stone steps leads up to the tombs of some of the Shoguns. Most of these tombs are striking for their austere simplicity, everything about them being suggestive of power, in striking contrast to the lavish decorations of the temples in front.

About a mile farther on is a very curious Buddhist temple, the burial-place of the forty-seven Ronins, who are looked upon as national heroes by the Japanese, and form the groundwork of one of the most popular romances. Although the events are said to have occurred only about two hundred years ago, they take a place in Japanese romance not unlike that of the heroes of King Arthur's Round Table amongst ourselves. The outlines of the story are

worth telling, as illustrating the national spirit, which elevated a bloodthirsty revenge to the highest place among the social virtues. The story is briefly this :

One Daimio having been assassinated by another in a dastardly manner, his vassals, or Samurai, as they are called (a position somewhat resembling that of the esquires and retainers of a mediæval knight), having now no liege lord, became Ronins, that is, 'wave men,' a kind of mendicant soldiers of fortune, it being beneath their dignity to engage in manual labour. Forty-seven of them entered into a secret league to avenge their lord's death, in which enterprise, after many romantic adventures, they finally succeeded; and having seized the great Daimio, they offered him what was considered an honourable end, by permitting him to perform harakiri, that is, to give himself the happy despatch by using his own short sword. On his refusal they slew him, and then, proceeding to Yedo, gave themselves up to the authorities, who sentenced the whole of them to perform harakiri, which accordingly they did, and have been looked upon as loyal heroes and martyrs ever since.

Pilgrimages are made to their tombs in this temple, as to the shrine of Thomas à Becket; incense is continually burned in their honour, and their clothes and relics, carefully preserved, are at certain intervals of years exhibited to the admiring crowds who flock from all parts of the country, as in Europe to the Holy Coat of Trèves, bringing great wealth to the temple Sengekuji.

This group of buildings in Shiba is one of the most remarkable in the whole country, surpassed only by those of Nikko and Kioto. But what struck me most was the wonderfully artistic arrangement of the trees. We seemed to be wandering in a wild wood full of exotic trees, and at every turn came unexpectedly on a roof nestled beneath them, with its upturned corners resplendent in the sunlight.

Few things can give the stranger a better idea of the art and manufactures of Japan than a visit to the Shiba Kwankoba, or bazaar, with its winding maze of corridors, on either side of which all the goods are exposed. It is well to visit this place with a well-lined purse, for the temptations are irresistible. The young ladies in attendance stand in front of, not behind, the counters. There is one immense advantage to the Western stranger, in that, contrary to the almost universal custom of the country, all the articles are marked in plain Japanese figures, and there is no bargaining. Hours may be spent in the contemplation of things new and old—antique carving in ivory; costly bits of ancient pottery; lacquer of every kind, ancient and modern; bewildering piles of delicate porcelain; silks, rich, plain, and embroidered; screens and fans; to say nothing of more homely domestic articles. I was able to make an interesting collection of Japanese tools and instruments, and many charming models illustrating all the operations of agriculture and carpentry, culinary work, and the life of the home. Dolls and toys were a great feature, and in the latter the productions of Holland pale before those of Tokio. One was instantly impelled to count up the numbers of nephews, nieces, and grandchildren whose birthdays would be gladdened by a remembrance from the other side of the world.

The following morning, April 29, on looking out I was surprised to see a display of colour in a novel form in every direction over the whole city. On the roofs and corners of houses all around were huge paper balloons in the gaudiest colours, suspended from bamboos from twenty to fifty feet high. The balloons, or hollow paper bags, are cut in the shape of a fish, sometimes twelve feet long, with a large open mouth formed by a wire ring, into which the wind blowing inflates the fish, which waves about after the manner of a weathercock, and is painted very cleverly in brilliant colours. It was the Japanese May Day, and on this day it is the custom that a paper fish should float over every house in which a boy has been born during the past year, and it remains hoisted for a month, giving every town and village the appearance of being *en fête*. The girls, I am ashamed to say, have no such honour paid to them. The explanation of this extraordinary custom is that it symbolises that as the fish swims up stream, so may the boy successfully face all the struggles of life. Some boys are honoured by a row of a dozen fishes on one pole, and certainly, to judge by the thousands of these fish-flags, there is no fear of a lack of men in the coming generation to defend their country.

I had been asked by the Tokio Christian Evidence

Society to deliver a lecture on this afternoon on Historic Corroborations of the Pentateuch from recent Egyptian discoveries. The society is formed by the missionaries of the various denominations, chiefly American, and the president is Archdeacon Shaw, the venerable senior missionary of the Society for the Propagation of the Gospel. The lecture-room was a large isolated hall, called the Tabernacle, built near the University by American Methodist Episcopals, but which is used freely for Christian work by all denominations. Archdeacon Shaw was in the chair, and I was rather taken aback by the size of the audience, about a thousand, of whom one-fourth were undergraduates of the University with their soft square caps. Most of them understand some English, and all are eager to improve themselves in our language. I also here met for the first time Bishop Hare, an American prelate, who was for the time assisting Bishop Williams. I must say the Japanese are patient listeners, for they bore with me for an hour and twenty minutes. I can only hope that many of them carried away a clearer idea than did the reporters of the Yokohama papers, which honoured me with a column. However, it is something that the Japanese papers should give unasked so much space to a religious subject. In the evening I enjoyed an extremely pleasant dinner-party at the English Bishop Bickersteth's, where I met, amongst others, Mr. Kirkwood, the legal adviser of the Japanese Government on international law, and Professor Ijima, Professor of Zoology in the University of Tokio.

While staying with Mr. Williams in Tsukiji I had my first and only experience of a Japanese earthquake. Would that the experience of others had been fraught with as little injury as my own! As I was sitting in my room just after breakfast, all of a sudden the floor seemed to heave a sigh; the prints, of which there were a good many, clattered two or three times on the walls, and the bells in the house began to ring. I knew at once what was the matter, for though it was years since I had felt an earthquake, the sensation is one the memory of which time can never efface. My mind reverted at once to the earthquake which overthrew Bona and Djileli in Algeria, and of which I had experienced the full force in the Sahara. On both occasions I had a strange physical sensation, resembling, I suppose, that of sea-sickness, of which happily I am personally ignorant. I do not suppose that the tremulous motion lasted more than three seconds, though the vibration continued a little longer. No further harm was done in Tokio, though people, when other conversation failed, mentioned it as we might the weather.

A Sunday in Tokio gave me an opportunity of seeing a little of the Christian mission work. Certainly the metropolis of Japan has samples before it of every form and development of Christianity. There are representatives of the Church Missionary Society, the first English society of any denomination to enter Japan; of the Society for the Propagation of the Gospel; Bishop Bickersteth's mission; the Cowley Fathers; the American Protestant Episcopal Church, very strongly represented; and of Americans, Presbyterian, Cumberland and Southern; Congregationalist; Baptist; Methodist Episcopal; Wesleyan; Dutch Reformed; Society of Friends; American Unitarian; Russo-Greek; and Roman of different orders. At this time I do not think there were any British Nonconformists.

I began with the Japanese morning service in the Church Missionary Society's church at Tsukiji. The congregation amounted to about sixty adults, and the sermon was preached by a young catechist who struck me as being well satisfied with himself. This, however, can hardly be called a mission church, as the native congregation bear the whole expense and maintain the catechist. I afterwards attended English service at the American cathedral. As we entered the building we met the Japanese congregation just streaming out. I was introduced to the venerable Bishop Williams, who had just resigned his see, a pleasing old man with humility and self-sacrifice stamped in every feature and action. He certainly was no lordly prelate. Prayers were read by a young clergyman, who had been in England with the Cowley Fathers. It is a noble church, cruciform, with aisles, lofty and light, and thoroughly Protestant in all its arrangements, perhaps more so than in its *personnel*, and serves all the English-speaking people in the concession.

At two o'clock I went to the Church Missionary Society's Japanese Sunday school, where the children repeated Hebrews xi., which of course formed a

capital text for Old Testament catechising. At three
o'clock began another Japanese service, at which I
did not stay long, but went in the evening for a long
walk with Mr. Williams to visit some of his preaching
places in the poorest parts of this vast city. He has
four in all, some of them miles apart. The first we
visited opens on a narrow street, its front being
simply paper shutters, which, when pushed back,
open the whole room on to the street. It is used
as a ragged school all the week, and as a Sunday
school, and in it are held continued preachings on
Sunday and weekday evenings; exhortations, short
or long (for the Japanese are patient listeners), being
given by one native after another. It has benches
for about sixty children. The farther half of the
room is a raised daïs, covered with fine Japanese
matting, and has a table in front. The few women
present sat on the matting. Sunday school was just
over when we arrived. A hymn was given out and
started in front of the room. This soon drew a crowd,
and the preaching began. The people looked very
attentive, the room quickly filled, and hardly any
went away as long as we were there. After another
hymn a second preacher stood up, very fluent and
energetic, his language to me all unknown, though,
as I afterwards found, I was used as an object-lesson,
which explained some broad grins turned towards me
once or twice. We then walked on for a mile to
another similar preaching place, where we found a
very earnest catechist addressing about a score of
men, who seemed to hang on his words. After him

came forward a well-dressed native gentleman, who spoke, Bible in hand, for nearly half an hour. He is a well-to-do business man and an earnest Christian, who regularly preaches on Sunday. After an hour's walk we got home at past ten o'clock, I having listened in whole or part to six Japanese sermons in one day.

I afterwards had opportunities of seeing the work of Bishop Bickersteth's mission in the Shiba district. Of course his staff is much larger and more concentrated than that of any other mission in Tokio, except perhaps the American Episcopal. He had living with him in his house, known as St. Andrew's, five young university clergymen, who devote their energies to educational and evangelistic work, the most important part of which is a Divinity School, where young natives are trained for the ministry. There are large classes held in the evening, which attract many besides the divinity students, and so outsiders and non-Christians are won. The missionaries certainly work very hard and zealously, and the result is seen in their converts. Close to the house is a pretty little church, in which there are many services throughout the day, of what appeared to an old-fashioned English Churchman an extreme type. I enjoyed many of the short services, though I could not but regret that such Romish names as Sext and Compline were given to the two English daily services, in which the prayers and all else were good and scriptural.

A few hundred yards from St. Andrew's and its little group of buildings is St. Hilda's, picturesquely situated on the side of a beautifully wooded little ravine, the home of an English sisterhood which has been established there by Bishop Bickersteth, and where much work is going on. Especially are there many classes for girls, all of good social position. Though by far the greater number of them are non-Christians, yet all have religious teaching, and under it some have become Christians. Attached to the school, but separated by a part of the garden, was a hospital for the poor, of twenty beds, beautifully ordered, and no lack of space and air, and under the management of a very clever and capable nurse. This hospital, I am sorry to learn, has lately been abandoned, owing to a difficulty about the lease. But we must remember that in Japan, with its medical schools and educated surgeons, there is not the demand for Medical Missions that exists in other Oriental countries.

During our stay at Tokio we had occasion to revisit Yokohama on business, and were fortunate enough to see in harbour there a finer fleet of men-of-war than can often be seen out of the Mediterranean. Not only was the Japanese fleet mustered there, several of them first-class warships, looking as trim and smart as any English man-of-war, but there were also riding at anchor a German frigate, a French frigate, a United States gunboat, and three English corvettes, with a Russian close behind them. It is remarked that an English man-of-war is never seen in these seas without a Russian in her train. Of all the five nationalities whose flag was shown, the

Japanese were by no means the least smart in appearance, though they certainly failed in rowing with the neatness that marked our gigs. The Russian looked very shabby, and certainly seemed wanting in smartness and cleanliness. Besides these, there were many mail liners and several magnificent American clippers, the first I had seen in these seas. It was difficult to realise, as we looked at this fleet of many nations, that we were in a roadstead unknown to name or fame five-and-twenty years ago.

After enjoying our row amongst the shipping, we found not a less strange contrast with the past on shore It was a gala day at Yokohama, and flags were flying in all directions, for the annual races were being held on the Bluff, and the Mikado had come down expressly to see this English sport. Oh, the descent in one generation, from the offspring of the gods enshrined in mystery amidst the enchanted gardens of Kioto, to the spruce gentleman in European costume, driving in his barouche to witness an English horse race!

FOREST TREES NEAR NIKKO.

CHAPTER III

A VISIT TO NIKKO

OUR first expedition into the interior from Tokio was to Nikko, nearly a hundred miles north of the capital. Nikko, which may be compared to the Oxford and Canterbury of the country combined, is, according to the firm belief of every Japanese, the most beautiful place in the world. They have a familiar proverb, 'No one can say Kekko, *i.e.* splendid, till you have been to Nikko,' and I am almost inclined to agree with them. Even before the introduction of railways, and when the journey could only be performed by the tedious and fatiguing jinriksha conveyance, no traveller who had the time at his command neglected to visit Nikko. Now it is as easy as any journey in England. We proceed by the great arterial railway of Japan as far as Utsu-no-Miya, whence a branch line, thirty miles in length, deposits us within two miles of the little town. In this journey for the first, but not for the last, time we felt the luxury of our extensive passport, by which we avoided the irritating necessity of making repeated applications to the central authorities at Tokio, stating beforehand the exact route proposed to be taken, the object of the journey, and the precise time to be occupied. The respect this passport commanded from the ubiquitous little policeman was apt to engender a triumphant feeling of superiority over ordinary mortals.

Our second-class carriage was clean and airy, the compartments opening into one another, and passengers often changing their seats. Our fellow-travellers appeared to be all thorough gentlefolk, several of them speaking English, and eager to air their knowledge. We could not but be amused at the solitary instance of superior exclusiveness which was exhibited by a very smart cavalry officer, no doubt a Japanese representative of 'the Tenth' of former days. More than one passenger, who evidently recognised that my daughter was engaged in missionary work, asked questions on the subject; and one especially seemed greatly interested, exchanged cards with her, and promised us a visit at the Nikko hotel where we intended to stay. The pace of the train happily was not that of an English express, so that we were enabled to enjoy the ever-varying landscape. Sometimes we passed through rice flats, more often along gentle slopes dotted with picturesque villages; amongst them a long straggling village entirely occupied by florists, who supply the Tokio market; whose gardens and nurseries, bright and pretty, set off the landscape with their rich borders of varying colours. We generally had in sight the old great northern road, one of the finest in the empire, lined with pines, cryptomerias, and other trees.

From Utsu-no-Miya, where we changed trains, the line was generally a steep ascent. In the last fifteen miles we rose 1,750 feet, and had a magnificent view of the mountain mass at the roots of which nestles Nikko. The train crept up parallel with a magnificent avenue of gigantic cryptomerias, which for twenty-five miles shade the ancient road by which the Shoguns annually visited the temples of Nikko. These trees and those of the various minor avenues about the temples are amongst the finest specimens of forestry in the world, averaging a hundred feet in height, many of them more, and some five or six feet in diameter at six feet from the ground. Although of such great size, they are, as our illustration shows, planted very close together, and form to the eye a mighty wall of dark green, through which not a ray of light penetrates, excepting where here and there some storm has overthrown one of these forest giants. We passed through many smaller woods of deciduous trees, brightened by the conspicuous bloom of two species of red azaleas and of three kinds of *Pyrus japonica*, one of which, which bears the largest flower, runs along the ground after the manner of the whortleberry. I was struck here, as I repeatedly was afterwards, by the wonderful variety of low flowering shrubs in the flora of Japan, and the comparative paucity of herbaceous flowers or annuals. A few miles before reaching Nikko, a second of these colossal avenues converges towards the railway, shading an ancient sacred road, by which the envoy of the Mikado used to carry his offerings to the shrines of the deceased heroes.

From the terminus of the railway we had a jinriksha ride of more than two miles through the village to our native hotel, Nikko being a long hilly street, lined on both sides with irregularly straggling houses. Let it not be supposed, however, that Nikko lacks a large hotel, built in foreign style and with all the usual accompaniments. We, however, wisely determined to go to a native hotel, and subsequent experience confirmed the correctness of our choice. After passing through the village we reached a rocky ravine spanned by two bridges side by side: a mountain torrent, now milky from the melted snow, dashed amongst the boulders at the bottom, and the sides were garnished with shrubs of many kinds, springing from every fissure in the cliffs. We crossed by the lower bridge. The other, a few yards above, is an ingenious wooden structure painted bright red, and forms a graceful elliptic curve. It is supported by massive stone piers fixed into the cliffs below, and its bright colour forms a striking contrast to the deep green of the tall cryptomerias which overhang it on either side. It is near a hundred feet long, and was built more than two hundred and fifty years ago, and we were told that such are the preservative qualities of the paint, or rather red lacquer, with which it is covered, that it has never required repair since its erection. A tall gate encloses it at either end, and it is only opened twice in the year for the passage of pilgrims visiting the shrine. It was formerly closed to all excepting the Shogun when he came to worship.

Its sanctity arises from its standing on the spot where Shodo Shonin, a mythical Japanese saint, is said to have crossed the river in the year A.D. 762. His story is full of strange, weird legends, of which

BRIDGES NEAR NIKKO.
(*The more distant is only opened twice in the year, for the passage of pilgrims.*)

the one connected with this bridge is a sample. Shodo is said to have been directed in a dream to ascend a certain mountain, but when he arrived at this spot he found his progress arrested by this impassable gorge. Falling on his knees and praying for help, a divine being of gigantic size flung across the river two green and blue snakes, which formed in an instant a bridge of rainbow shape spanning the ravine. The moment the saint had crossed, the god and the snake-bridge vanished. Shodo then settled at this spot and erected a hut, which was the forerunner of the group of magnificent temples which are now the glory of Japan. Shodo Shonin died in 817, and he seems to have been a Shinto devotee, who, meeting some Chinese missionaries, embraced the Buddhist faith, or rather incorporated it with his hereditary religion.

Crossing the bridge, we turn sharp round to the left, up a gentle ascent flanked on either side by little villas ensconced in their gardens, till at length a little board projecting neatly from a garden hedge proclaims in Chinese and English characters our hotel, first patronised by Mrs. Bishop, the well-known pioneer lady. A tiny stream meanders through the tiny garden, with stepping-stones, islands, bridges, and quaintly dwarfed trees and shrubs, the trees the exact models of the willow pattern and other porcelain devices. On a broad stepping-stone in front of the verandah ledge of the cardboard house are two pairs of slippers for our use, and we step into the exquisitely clean, fine matting, soft as velvet, which carpets the rooms, while the boards of the verandah are polished as a dining-table. There are three parlours in a row, all open, for the sliding paper walls are pushed back into a recess or taken out in the daytime. One of these is our sitting-room. But as to the furniture, even into this exquisite gem of a Japanese house foreign ideas have penetrated. In consideration of the weakness of Western travellers, there is a little table and two cane chairs in each room, for all are furnished precisely alike. There is also a tiny side-table, and on each table is a vase of lovely flowers, and the sides of each room are occupied by cupboards with sliding paper doors. Behind these rooms is a similar arrangement of open verandah, looking out on another garden of dwarf trees, islands, and bridges, but bounded by a steep cliff overhung, as is all the mountain-side, with forest trees, and down the cliffs are arranged a series of baby cascades, which feed the tiny lakes and then pass under the house in a porcelain channel into the front garden. The paper sides of the rooms are hung with many kakemono, depicting very cleverly groups of birds or scenery. Lacquered and varnished stairs lead from back and front verandahs to our bedrooms, having paper partitions which are thrown back until the evening. The dwelling apartments of our host and his family are a continuation of our own, and are reached by the same verandah, the kitchen, which we often visited, separating them. In these private rooms we found the same exquisite matting with which the guest-room floors were covered, but no tables and chairs.

Our host, to whom we had already written for apartments, received us with all the ceremony and grace of a Japanese gentleman, showed us our rooms upstairs and down, though, as we were for the present the only guests, we enjoyed the run of the whole house. Mr. Kanaya was a typical host, making us feel at once that we were looked upon not as lodgers by payment, but as guests of the family. Like a Boniface of the olden time, he accompanied us into our parlour, sat gracefully on the floor, and entered into conversation, recounted his recollections of Mrs. Bishop, suggested the excursions which ought not to be omitted, and the number of hours or days that each would occupy, and actually inquired whether the bent of our tastes were antiquarian, or botanical, or for scenery or sport. With his hotel he combined a small farm, and was also a lay clerk in the great Buddhist temple hard by. He volunteered a full account of himself and his family; but, knowing our religious opinions, he took care to inform us that, though he held office in the temple, for which he was remunerated, he did not believe much in Buddhism. In fact, he was, like many of his countrymen, more agreeable than reliable.

After chatting some time he reminded us that we were to be supplied with foreign dinner, and, of course, professed readiness to give any delicacy from any part of the world. Finally it was decided that we should have fish soup, a standing Japanese dish pigeons and pheasant, with Japanese sponge-cake and tea. This sponge-cake is a curious relic of the ancient Spanish connection. It is known by the

Japanese as Castera, *i.e.* Castille (the Japanese always substituting 'r' for 'l,' which is wanting in their language, and which they find great difficulty in pronouncing), the art of making which they learnt from the Spanish missionaries three hundred years ago. On my demurring to the pheasant and asking if it were not the close season, our host clapped his hands, and thus summoned the pretty little maiden, who soon reappeared with a beautiful green cock-pheasant, which had evidently been snared and illegally poached in anticipation of our visit. This bird, known as *Phasianus versicolor*, is in form and size exactly like our own, but its plumage a brilliant glossy green. It is very common in all parts of the country which we visited; as is another species with a very much longer and broader tail, of a rich copper colour, powdered with white spangles, known as the copper pheasant, *Phasianus scintillans*.

There was considerable alarm a few years ago lest these pheasants should have been exterminated by the demand for them in Paris, and I am afraid in England too, for the decoration of ladies' hats. One merchant at Yokohama told me that he had in one year exported thirty thousand copper-pheasant skins. Fortunately, the plumage of the hens being very modest, they were not in demand, and in three or four years the fashion happily passed away, though not before the government were proposing to interfere to arrest the destruction of the greatest ornament of the Japanese woods.

Having thus installed ourselves, we set out to take

a cursory survey of the neighbourhood. Retracing our steps towards the sacred bridge, we passed the foreign hotel, a large unsightly building in European style, when we were surprised at being hailed in English by old friends from Shanghai, whom we never expected to meet here, and whom we were delighted to have as companions in our subsequent excursions. Returning to our home at sunset, we found our paper walls all closed in for the night, and also, what I had not perceived before, that there are double walls, the outer one of wood, all round the verandah, and which during the daytime are put away in cupboards, but which now gave the house the appearance of a huge wooden box. They are certainly useful, not only for warmth, but for privacy, as the little boys are very fond of watching the proceedings, especially of foreigners, by wetting the paper walls with their tongues and with their fingers making peep-holes. However, the weight of the whole of these walls, whether wooden or paper, should be reckoned in ounces rather than pounds. I could almost fancy there was a danger, if anything caught the button of my coat, of walking away with the walls of the house.

The inspection of the group of the temples and Mausoleum of Iyeyasu is a full day's work. This latter is perhaps the finest, and certainly the most interesting historically, of the vast group of sacred buildings that dot the lower slopes of the mountain Nikko San. From the great repute for sanctity of Nikko, it was chosen as the burial-place of Iyeyasu, in the year 1617. This Iyeyasu was one of the greatest rulers and generals Japan has seen, and the founder of the Shogun dynasty of Tokugawa, which continued in unbroken succession the practical rulers of the country until the revolution of 1868, when the old feudal system of the rule of the Daimios under the Shogun or Mayor of the Palace was entirely abolished, and the Mikado, who had been for many centuries a mere *fainéant* monarch, like the later Merovingians of France, emerged from his sacred obscurity and became the actual monarch of the country; and in a few years established a constitutional government.

As Shogun, Iyeyasu was a simple usurper. Born in 1542, he had been a military officer under the Shogun Hideyoshi, for some time the patron and protector of the Christians. On the death of Hideyoshi, Iyeyasu rebelled against his youthful son, and, after a struggle lasting several years, was finally recognised as ruler. He immediately devoted himself to breaking up the power of the Daimios, compelling them, as feudal inferiors, to do homage to himself, whilst he surrounded the court of the Mikado with his own troops, and in fact confined him in a gilded prison. However unscrupulous may have been his methods, Japan owes to him the enjoyment of a really centralised government. He kept in his own hands many forts throughout the country which had hitherto been held by the Daimios; he made great arterial roads through the whole country; established a postal system; and enacted laws, which were to supersede the capricious and arbitrary internal rule of the Daimios on their estates. He was, for his age, a really scientific man, and a great patron of literature. In fact, his rule has been called the Renaissance epoch of Japan. But, on the other hand, he was the first to commence the bloody persecution of the Christians, which ended a few years after his death in the extermination of Christianity.

Under his direction the Daimios were required to compel all Christians to renounce their faith. This they resisted even to blood. At length they were forced to take up arms, and raised the standard of rebellion for the first time in Japanese history, for hitherto their wars had been rather faction fights than rebellions. The struggle continued for several years, from 1606 to 1615. For some time the Christians maintained their independence, until in 1611 Iyeyasu is said to have discovered a plot manipulated by the Spanish friars for reducing the country to a condition of subjection to Spain under a Christian viceroy. From that time all foreigners were expelled and the native Christians ruthlessly massacred. The capture of Osaka in 1615 was fatal to all hopes of success by the Christian party. The slaughter continued for several days, and the Jesuit historians assert that 100,000 men perished in this war. The struggle, however, continued for more than twenty years after Iyeyasu's death, and did not end until 1637, when the castle of Shimabara was taken, and 37,000 Christians massacred, and thousands of others hurled down the rocks previously mentioned in the harbour of Nagaski.

But enough of this digression, for we have long since arrived at Iyeyasu's mausoleum. It is, like all the others, a large enclosure surrounded by, and filled with, cryptomerias and other large trees, with stately avenues mounting up the steep hills on which they are placed. The temple is in no case a single building, but a group of some twenty temples, and this one has a gorgeous red pagoda in the wood outside, towering among the trees with admirable effect. On the outskirts are some fine houses and gardens fringing the avenue, into one of which we turned, having requested at the porter's lodge 'that we might be allowed humbly to raise our eyes to the landscape.' After noticing this interesting specimen of native horticulture, we turned back to the avenue, on the way up which are a series of lych-gate roofs with boards under them containing the names of contributors to the preservation fund of the temples, among them a board in English, explaining the appeal. Another in Japanese contained a record of the donations of English and American visitors.

Within the enclosure were all the characteristic features which we had noticed in the temples of Shiba, but on a much larger scale—colossal bronze lamps, bells, one of them rivalling the Russian castings; great monolith pillars, etc., the gifts of Corean, Loochoo, and other foreign monarchs. This was not the only place in which we found historic evidence of the claims of Japan to some kind of recognition by Corea.

Not the least interesting of the various structures

were three long halls adjoining each other, in which are exhibited the possessions, clothing, armour, furniture, and other articles used by Iyeyasu in his lifetime. These are silent witnesses of the intelligence and culture of the Japan of three hundred years ago, and show how much was due to the Spanish fathers. Among them I was much struck by an orrery, evidently of European make, and various astronomical instruments, and others, which well illustrate the practice of the art of navigation before the invention of the quadrant. Our guide, however, considered his swords, said to be of wonderfully tempered steel, as far more worth our study.

Arranged along the gallery over the cabinets in which these collections were kept, was a series of paintings illustrating falconry as carried on in Iyeyasu's time, for he was evidently a sportsman as well as a warrior and philosopher. We had in fact an illustrated history of the practice of the gentle art. The similarity of the hoods, jesses, and other falconer's gear, with those in use in Europe, was very remarkable, as we can hardly conceive that falconry in Japan was derived from a European source. At the same time I think we have presumptive evidence that European and Japanese hawking have been derived from a common original.

Perhaps I may be allowed to say a few more words on this subject, as falconry is, so far as I know, the only instance in historic times in which a European art is identical in all its methods with that of the Land of the Rising Sun. Investigation will probably

JAPANESE FALCONER.

show that Assyria was the cradle of an art that spread thence through the whole world, east and west. The earliest monumental record of falconry is a sculpture discovered by Sir Henry Layard at Khorsabad, representing a falconer with a hawk on his wrist. This is standing evidence that hawking was practised there at least as early as 1700 B.C. But Japanese records carry us back further still, for if they may be relied on, falconry was practised in China centuries previously. A Japanese historian, of whose work a French translation has been published, relates that falcons were amongst the Chinese presents made to princes in the time of the Hia Dynasty, supposed to have commenced 2205 B.C. We know from classical authors that falconry was practised in Central Asia, Persia, and India about 400 B.C.

There is no inconsiderable literature devoted to the art in the Japanese language. No fewer than fourteen treatises on the subject are enumerated by Harting in his *Bibliotheca Accipitraria*, many of them long anterior to the visits of the Spaniards. Amongst the minutiæ of the art, we may mention that, whilst European falconers repair broken feathers by what is called an imping needle, the Japanese repair a broken tail-feather by splicing on a new one with lacquer varnish. The Japanese writers on falconry mention the goshawk, the peregrine, the sparrow-hawk, the osprey, which they call the pike-catching hawk, the gier-falcon, which they obtain from Kamschatka, and, last and least, the grey shrike, which they have succeeded in training to catch small birds.

H

Hawking, however, since the revolution has become very much a thing of the past, and is almost extinct with the old feudal system, inasmuch as the new laws of trespass, which are very strict, preclude any, excepting the few who still possess great estates, from indulging in this pastime. Another reason of its decadence is probably the great increase in cultivation. From the series of pictures at Nikko we may infer that the goshawk was the favourite bird of Iyeyasu, for only one of them exhibited the prowess of the peregrine. Mr. Harting (to whose kindness I am indebted for permission to copy the illustration) infers, from the identity in almost every point of the practice of the falconers of the East and West, that the falconry of the whole world originated in India, and was introduced long before the historic period, by the Indo-Germanic race, from the plains of Hindustan.

But leaving the memorials and picture gallery of Iyeyasu, we observed at the entrance two curiously carved figures of elephants, the knowledge of which was probably brought with Buddhism. Close by is a magnificent sacred pine-tree, said to have been carried about by Iyeyasu in his palanquin, when it was still small enough to be in a flower-pot. Alongside of this is the stable of Buddha, open in front, with an unfortunate piebald sacred horse ready for him to ride when he returns to earth. The poor animal stands, tied up and caparisoned, with long rows of saucers full of beans just out of his reach, for each of which the devout pay five rin (*i.e.* one farthing) to give the tantalised steed. Its groom told us, however, that sometimes it is taken out for exercise. It reminds one of the sacred bull of the Egyptians. In another temple the nuns perform sacred dances, solemn and majestic, and are glad to receive a few sen (halfpennies).

One could spend hours in admiring the bold designs of animals and the grotesque carvings which enrich all the temples, both within and without, in bewildering confusion, in which dragons, unicorns, griffons and phœnixes of strange devices, enough to perplex the most skilled heraldic student, are mingled with lifelike representations of lions, cattle, monkeys, foxes, and other creatures of every-day life. In another building equally lavish in its ornamentation is the great library of Buddhist theological works. A flight of steps leads to the next group of temples. One of the peculiarities of Nikko is that all these groups of buildings are on terraces as it were, raised one above another, and connected by wide flights of steps with massive stone balustrades. On the next platform is a collection of royal gifts; and amongst the colossal lamps, bells, and stone lions is a great brass candelabrum of Dutch manufacture, which was pointed out as the feudal tribute paid by the King of Holland, who, they tell you, was one of the vassals of the Mikado. But it would be monotonous to describe the various temples and courtyards, or rather cloister garths and cathedral closes, which would repay the artistic connoisseur many days spent in careful examination.

We do not reach the tomb of Iyeyasu till we are at the summit of the small hill. It is of massive bronze, shaped like a small pagoda. Visitors are not allowed to enter within the small enclosure, although the whole of it can be seen. Vases of flowers and lighted tapers are continually renewed in front of it.

The grouping and arrangement of these temples suggested a good idea of what a Greek *temenos* must have been, such as those so familiar at Baalbec and elsewhere, although these occupy much greater space. We spent two or three days in visiting the other temple groups, which are all worth seeing. One large temple is called the Hall of Meditation. It is quite empty, save for one semi-colossal image of Buddha, but is surrounded by a very wide verandah, where the worshippers walk round and round for hours repeating the name of Buddha, and counting the repetitions on their rosaries. In all these temples the enormous wooden roof, carved with all sorts of figures and rich in gilt and paint, is the most striking feature. The wonderful carved work and lacquer furnishing of these structures occupy pages and pages of the guide-books, and are interwoven with the history of Japan for many centuries back. It is the Valhalla of the nation, and the traveller who wishes to be inspired with the spirit of old Japan must make his sojourn at Nikko, and not at Tokio.

Though many thousand natives annually visit Nikko as pilgrims, yet amongst all the crowds which we saw there seemed to be very little worship and no enthusiasm. They stroll quietly about like sightseers in Durham Cathedral, and drop a rin ($\frac{1}{20}$ penny) here and there into a box. The only shrines that apparently created devotion were those of the God of Wealth, represented by a fat man with a huge sack on his back, sitting on two great sacks of rice, and grinning. He gets abundance of rin, candles, and prayers. I should explain that in most of the temples there are many little shrines exactly corresponding to the side altars of Romish worship, which are dedicated to numerous popular or local deities, evolved partly from distorted traditions of Shintoism, and partly from the many incarnations of Buddha.

Another popular deity is the God of Strength, who is represented with enormous arms and calves. His shrine was heaped with offerings of pairs of tiny clogs and old sandals, and his devotees pray to him that their calves may develop muscles as strong as his. He is the popular deity of the jinriksha men. In one very rich temple three colossal wooden statues were conspicuous, painted respectively red, green, and blue. The green monster was the God of Wind, carrying the winds, like Æolus, in a bag. The God of Thunder was red, hurling a thunderbolt, very like a statue of Jupiter. The third figure is, I believe, a representation of a mythological protector of Buddha. This temple struck me as one of the most beautiful, largely owing to the effect of the magnificent cryptomerias and noble rhododendrons grouped around it.

The wonderful temples and collection of Japanese art are not the only attractions of Nikko. For any one sound in wind and limb it is an admirable centre for excursions. In every direction we found long and lovely walks up the valleys, with mountains towering above, their summits still covered with snow, and their lower slopes painted with the pink and crimson bloom of trees of various kinds, some of them unknown to me. Turning round in our scrambles, we looked down on mountain streams dashing over the boulders, while the ground of the open forest was covered with the bright red flowers of the creeping *Pyrus japonica*, varied by the sombre clusters of dog-violet. We could scarcely go a mile without coming across waterfalls, any one of which would have made the fortune of a German or a Swiss pleasure resort.

A very interesting but not long expedition is that to Kamman-ga-fuchi, by a path up the river-side. Half an hour from Nikko by the roadside, just fronting the river, was the most exquisite little miniature park and house with a little shrine, all in perfect order; in every respect a typical Japanese gem. Attached to it was a tea-house, the landlady of which showed us about, presented us with bouquets of flowers, and, seeing I was interested in her horticulture, with true national courtesy took me round, giving me the Japanese names of the various shrubs. This was all done without any expectation of a *douceur*, which when offered was waved back with the expression *Do itashimashite?* or 'What have I done?' though eventually accepted.

The path follows along for some distance the winding course of the stream, till we arrived at

STONE BUDDHAS NEAR NIKKO.

Kamman-ga-fuchi, where, ranged on the other side of the river, are a long row of images of Buddha, about a hundred in number. Nothing is known authentically of their origin or meaning, but we were told that it is impossible to count them accurately, and that however often the feat is attempted, the conclusion is always different. This superstition is not peculiar to Japan, for the same thing is said of various circles of Druidical stones in England.

Although without a history, a visit to these Buddhas, and the lovely, if not grand, scenery, amply repays the walk. Not the least interesting to me was the introduction it afforded me to many of the native birds for the first time. The Japanese ornithology is peculiarly interesting to a British naturalist, from its close resemblance to, as well as its marked difference from, our British fauna. The most conspicuous and attractive bird in this walk was the Japanese pied wagtail (very much larger, and with the black and white in its plumage more strikingly contrasted than in our own), which continually flitted across our path, or ran in the road in front of us. The trees and shrubs were ceaselessly visited by little flocks of various kinds of titmice, some identical with, and others very close to, our own. Family parties of the schoolboy's favourite, the long-tailed or bottle tit, were seldom absent from view. The representative of the great tit, with exactly the same note as our own, the marsh and the cole were everywhere in evidence; and the conspicuous chestnut, black, and white titmouse (*Parus varius*) peculiar to Japan, and its favourite cage-bird, was most abundant of all.

Leaving what I call the glen of the Buddhas, we mounted the hill by a not too steep ascent and visited various cascades, whose quaint Japanese names I need not inflict upon my readers, but which may be translated, one as the 'vermicelli cascade,' another as the 'mist falling,' a very appropriate name; and another as the 'pillow cascade,' why so named I know not. All these have a fall of from fifty to sixty feet, and at the time of our visit were unusually fine, owing to the melted snow. We were rather too early for the botany, but there were already many interesting ferns unfolding their fronds, several of which, especially an aspidium, were entirely new to me. But in every department of natural history, the birds, the butterflies, the fishes, the botany, the same difficulty arises. Everything bears a strong resemblance to the fauna and flora of Europe, and yet almost always there is a difference, less so perhaps in the birds than in anything else. That laughing, screaming jay among those maples overhead, you would say, was undoubtedly our own jay to the minutest particular, and yet if you were to handle him, he is different, but only by a black streak from his beak to his eye, where our jay is chestnut. And so the bullfinch, identical at first sight with our bird-fancier's darling and gardener's abomination, voice, flight, nest, and eggs undistinguishable; but we shall always find the native of Japan with a ruddy tinge on the back, and less decisive red on the breast, yet bullfinch all the world over. And so with the butterflies. Though the characteristic forms of Japan often rival the Indian in splendour, and infinitely surpass our own in variety, these do not appear till the summer is further advanced; but our ramble was enlivened by the hovering of familiar acquaintances, especially the common cabbage white and pale clouded yellow. These two species are identical with our own. Along with these, but in sparser numbers, were representatives of our early spring friends, an orange tip and a brimstone.

Our next expedition was very much longer, and was one of the most charming rambles which we enjoyed in the whole country. It was to the Lake of Chusenji. We had to make an early start, for it is a five hours' walk and a steady ascent nearly the whole way, through wild scrub and forest, the whole of which is an imperial preserve where Nature has full sway; though I fear that in Japan, as in England, the genus poacher exists in spite of royal and imperial edicts. As we left the road which for a mile or two we had traversed yesterday, and entered a pathway up the hillside, a large notice slab attracted our attention, warning the visitor that the killing or snaring of living things in any manner was forbidden by imperial command. I am afraid it does not speak well for the reputation of our countrymen that half-way up, at the tea-house where travellers halt, we found a similar notice in English as well as in the vernacular.

Our path lay by the edge of a deep gorge, with a

swollen stream dashing far beneath, and for the first four miles cultivated ground intermingled with coppice. The front seemed to be barred by a snow-capped volcanic mountain range with many jagged peaks, the highest of which, Nantaizan, is laid down as 8,300 feet. Men were fishing in the most tempting-looking trout pools, and rapidly filling their creels from the milky turbid water with a kind of trout, with crimson bellies and silver spots. These sportsmen were courteous and friendly, and proud to exhibit their tackle, which was really very clever. Their rods were simple bamboo stems. They had a good assortment of flies in little boxes, among them salmon flies, made of what seemed to me golden pheasant feathers. They told me they used these in the lake above, though the river seemed an arduous one for the most agile of salmon to attempt. I was told that there is abundance of salmon in the lake, but this was not the season for them. The streams are well stocked with smaller fry of various species, which I will not attempt to name. We soon began to climb the steep mountain-side by a rough path, occasionally cut for a long distance out of the cliff, high above the stream. We were in a forest of cryptomeria, pine, fir (*Abies tsuga*), maple, alder, oak, birch, and larch, not yet in leaf.

The gigantic cryptomerias were a grand sight, and occasionally a tall fir towered above all the surrounding hard-wood trees. But with few exceptions the deciduous trees and ferns were only just budding. I here saw the Japanese robin and hedge-sparrow for the first time, both very like our own, and exactly resembling them in note and habits, though in Japan they are both exclusively mountain birds, said never to be found lower than 4,000 feet, and consequently are the rarest of Japanese birds in collections. One large tree, not in leaf, but covered with sheets of large rosy blossoms of an open trumpet shape, monopetalous, called by our men the yasu, we could not make out. It only grows at a considerable altitude, and, in fact, generally the unmelted snow carpeted the ground where it was in flower. Here it was so abundant as to make up for the want of foliage in the other trees, and contrasted beautifully with the dark firs and cryptomerias. There were plenty of species of thuyas and other smaller trees strange to me. One of the most striking features of this forest were the festoons of a long trailing moss (*Lycopodium Sieboldi*), which with its tendrils forms fleecy pendants from each bough, and at a distance these have the effect of a silvery mist enveloping the tree.

Some fine cascades varied the scene, and here and there a châlet-like tea-house was perched on the edge of a bluff commanding some fine view of a waterfall or ravine. We halted at more than one of them, and enjoyed green tea at half a farthing a cup, with a morsel of green bean cake and a sugar-plum thrown in. The situation of these tea-houses is another instance of the inborn love of natural beauty so characteristic of the people. On a moist bank behind one of these tea-houses I found large clumps of

Primula japonica, and it was interesting to note that the colours were as varied in the wild as in the cultivated specimens in our gardens, though possibly these may have been stragglers from cultivation.

The road or track had been washed away in many places by recent floods, and we often had to pass and repass the stream by what seemed perilously slender bamboo and straw foot-bridges, which, as they had no hand-rails, demanded all one's nerve to make a safe passage, the bridge being simply three or four very long bamboos thrown across the gully, and wisps of rice straw plaited between them. But we soon found that they were not difficult to use, so long as only one passenger at a time attempts the feat, the straw wisps affording a foot-hold that, at least, does not slip. Perhaps they are not more permanent than the plaited straw sandals, or *waraji*, which strew the paths everywhere, and which can be bought for a penny a pair at every wayside shop and tea-house, and which last but a few days, and are then flung aside, the wearer being equally at home with or without his sandals. Towards the end of a long day I often felt sorely tempted to discard my heavy European shoes and, slitting the end of my stocking, to adopt the light and airy waraji, which is only fastened by a couple of wisps passing between the great and other toes, and then round the ankle.

A less steep but far more circuitous road to the sacred lake was being constructed, and several times intersected our path. It was evidently engineered with great skill, for this is a science to which the

Japanese have applied themselves with great energy and success. The horses employed in the cuttings for drawing the trolleys were all shod, not with iron shoes, but with straw sandals like their masters, fastened on like the leather slippers which our horses wear in drawing lawn-mowers. This was not the only new road in course of construction, for the whole neighbourhood of Nikko was as full of road repairing as though a new County Council had just come into office. On inquiring why so much was being done to the roads, we were informed that as the honourable visit of the great Czarovitch of Russia was looked for in a few weeks, they wished to have all the roads in the best possible condition, and a considerable sum was being spent on them. Owing, however, to the untoward event to be mentioned later on in our rambles, the imperial visit to Nikko was never accomplished.

At length we arrive at the Lake of Chusenji, a great mountain tarn, in a wide mountain amphitheatre, the steep slopes of which are thickly wooded everywhere to the water's edge. It is about eight miles long and not quite three wide, about 4,500 feet above the sea. The road suddenly opens upon one end of the lake, affording a view along its whole length. We proceed through a long wooden village, with a monotonous row of sheds or huts on one side, all shut up, the lodgings of the pilgrims who crowd to this holy place in summer. The Shinto temple is said to have been founded by Shodo Shonin a thousand and eighty years ago, and the grounds are looked upon as sacred, and can only be entered on foot. The side of the village nearest the lake before one reaches the temple is lined with shops and teahouses, provided with charming balconies overhanging the lake, and with a lovely view of the mountains; and beneath boats lie idly moored, irresistibly inviting us to an excursion.

Here we were treated in real country fashion. Our guest-chamber on the first floor was one with the verandah overhanging the calm blue waters, and on the matting we sat. Brightly clad damsels carried tiny square lacquer tables, about six inches high, which they set before us, but considerately supplied us with *futon* (wadded quilts rolled up) on which to lean; a delicate consideration for our Western uncouthness. One little table was set before each guest, on which were little saucers of exquisite mountain trout, seaweed soup, and—the one delicacy which we never could be brought to endure—daikon, a sort of decayed radish. These delicacies, however, we supplemented by substantials brought from the valley below. After a rest of two or three hours we investigated the sights of the place, and returned by a slightly different route, which enabled us to see another fine cascade, 350 feet. It was dark long before we had reached our delicious little inn, thoroughly tired and as thoroughly happy. We found our arrival awaited by a circle of vendors of curios, lacquer-ware, bronzes, photos, and bird-skins, for our fame had evidently spread, visitors being very rare at this time of year. But not even the bird-skins could keep us awake, and we promptly retired to our well-earned rest.

During the night we were occasionally roused by the sound as of the swish of a dozen shower-baths combined, but our little wooden doll-house, thin as were its boards, turned the rain well. So deep were

LAKE OF CHUSENJI.

the eaves that in the morning we found even the verandahs dry, though the rain ceased not the whole day. It was the first wet day I had had in Japan, and I only had one more during my visit, and it also was a Sunday. To take a walk was out of the question, but our friends from the foreign hotel joined us for morning service, as well as a young native, a friend of our landlord, and, so far as we knew, the only Christian in Nikko. He was an intelligent young man who often came in to offer his services as interpreter if required, or to tell us the traditions of the place. He had been five years in California, where he had joined the Christian Church and been baptized. He had settled here as a teacher of English. That a young man of superior position can find it worth while to establish himself in a small, out-of-the-way country town as a teacher of English, shows the rapidity with which the study of our language is advancing.

In fact, as I shall have occasion to mention later, the only foreign languages that seem to have any attraction for this people are English and Chinese. The latter most naturally, as it is the vehicle through which they have received all their religious and moral teaching, for the aboriginal religion of Shintoism has no literature, and the Buddhist classics which are studied are in the Chinese language; while their whole moral teaching is based upon Confucianism, all the treatises on which are in the same tongue. It should be understood that in Japanese literature the characters used are Chinese, the inflections and particles being added in the Japanese syllabary, or *kana*, as it is called. The Chinese being an uninflected language, and structurally utterly distinct from Japanese, the latter have adopted the Chinese sign for the root-word, to which they affix *kana* or syllabic signs as may be required. Moreover, before the opening of the country to foreigners they had some external and diplomatic dealings with China, which rendered the language a useful accomplishment both to the statesman and the merchant. All these facts have led to the incorporation of many Chinese words in the learned language, though their pronunciation would be unintelligible to a Chinaman. With the opening of the country to trade, to foreign inventions, and to modern science, has arisen the necessity for a limitless addition of scientific terms to the language. To meet this want the Japanese have never adopted English words, but have gone to Chinese, exactly as we do to Greek for terms relating to steam, electricity, navigation, and the like.

Our visitor evidently enjoyed the service, though perhaps a somewhat lukewarm Christian. Yet how, as he remarked, could his faith do otherwise than 'get thin,' according to the Japanese idiom, when alone, without one fellow-believer to sympathise with him, in this very centre of Japanese Buddhism!

In the afternoon the clouds still continued their ceaseless downpour, and my daughter succeeded in gathering in our parlour, out of which the table and two chairs were cleared, a little company of the young Christian, the wife, family, and servants of Mr. Kanaya, our landlord, and several of the neighbours. They all sat round the room on the mats, my daughter, in the centre, reading and explaining by means of Scripture pictures the Gospe story, and keeping up their eager attention for a couple of hours.

Mr. Kanaya, as a member of the choir of one of the Buddhist temples, supplied me with a set of altar furniture in bronze which had become his perquisite on being replaced by a newer set. They would almost have served for a Romish altar, consisting of two candlesticks, a pair of flower-vases, a paten for rice, a small incense censer, and a little acolyte's bell. In addition, I obtained a set of Buddhist priest's robes, the cassock being light green, the alb represented by a pale drab vest, whilst an embroidered tippet would admirably do duty for a chasuble, and a green stole embroidered in gold completed the outfit. There is nothing new under the sun!

We spent another day in visiting other groups of temples, to describe which would be in the main a repetition of the former account; and afterwards walked up a magnificent avenue of cryptomerias shading a finely paved road. Many of the trees are seven feet in diameter, but their height is greater in proportion. We measured one of them by the simple method which I have often employed in calculating the height of ruins; that is, by using a long stick and comparing the length of its shadow with that of the tree, then calculating by proportion the height of the tree from the length of the stick. We found its height to be 160 feet. These trees are said to be the tallest in the world next to the sequoias of California. In the wood a number of very curious plants rewarded our research, especially a sort of giant Herb Paris, with three leaves instead of four—the badge of the Tokugawa Shogun family. But as it was only just in leaf, I had no means of ascertaining its botanical character. Every now and then

BUDDHIST PRIEST.

at the side of the path was a little niche scooped out in the rock, in which was placed a miniature little Buddha, very delicately carved in wood, some of them not more than six inches high, and the remains of a few tapers in front, recalling the little wayside shrines of Italy or Spain. I was sorely tempted to pocket one of these interesting relics, but did not feel myself justified in acting the iconoclast, though I argued that it might be a very efficient way of suppressing Buddhism.

Another charming little expedition was to the cascade of Nanataki. The walk afforded every variety of native scenery—dashing mountain torrents, rickety bamboo bridges, pine-woods, picturesque tea-houses, and fairy little gardens with their lakes and bridges, the former full of goldfish. Wherever a little rock or edge of a bluff offered a site with an attractive landscape, there was sure to be perched a tea-house. In a wood was a sequestered cemetery, where the ashes of those cremated are deposited under tiny obelisks. There was one new handsome obelisk with a long inscription, all picked out in red, and a toy shrine in front of it with bright flowers planted around. The red paint signifies that the hero of the monument is still living, for those who can afford it like to put them up and inscribe their epitaphs in their lifetime. At length we reached a tea-house on the top of a hill, and from it looked down into the next valley, with a fine waterfall, perhaps 200 feet high. I was content with the distant prospect, though the proper proceeding would have been to scramble down the steep side of the mountain, and then, despising the drenching from the spray, to get between the water and the cliff. As a naturalist my time was not wasted, for, whether it were yesterday's rain or this morning's bright sun, one or other had evoked a number of butterflies, who emerged for the first time from their chrysalides.

On our return we had, as usual, a levee of curio-mongers, and certainly our fastidiousness on former evenings had induced them to bring some really good bits of old bronze, etc. But most satisfactory to me was the return of a man and a boy who had brought a few bird-skins the first evening, and who had been evidently surprised by my taking the whole consignment. I had told the bearer to bring some more. On this occasion the collector himself appeared with his lad with between two and three hundred skins, very neatly made, all labelled and ticketed with Japanese name, place, and date. Recognising some of the labels as being of a type familiar to me at home, I inquired what he usually did with his birds. He explained that he had been for several years employed by an Englishman, who was now dead, to whom he used to send all he collected. I soon ascertained that he had been employed by the late Mr. H. Pryer, through whom I had obtained many specimens. Unfortunately the locality usually given had been Yokohama, whereas all these birds were collected in the forests round Nikko, and at a height of from three to eight thousand feet above the sea. No wonder that English writers have gone astray as to the localities of the birds of Japan. It was pretty much as if the dotterels and ring-ousels of Cross Fell should be labelled 'Obtained at Liverpool.' I found both him and his lad most intelligent and delightful enthusiasts. Along with the bird-skins were specimens of no less than five species of squirrel. The lad explained to me in word and pantomime the homes and habits of each species. Amongst them were two or three skins of a very large species, which he stated to me was found in summer only in the pine-forests near the mountain top; but in winter, during heavy snowstorms, he declared that, unlike any other kind, these creatures came down to the villages (we are speaking, of course, of villages of higher altitude than Nikko), and when they saw at night a light through the walls of a cottage, would break a hole through the paper, and, entering without ceremony, put out the candle and eat it. I give this story for what it is worth; but it certainly was not only vouched for by the lad and his employer, but attested by all the by-sitters. His collection comprised more than a hundred species of birds, but he had seldom brought more than a pair of each, all carefully sexed. I took them up one by one, and at once the note was imitated, and often the action of the bird, as in the case of the woodpeckers, with inimitable pantomime. Whether it were the jerking of the black water-ousel or dipper, the skimming of the swallow, the dash of the swift, the chatter of the jay, or the sudden whistle of the bush-warbler as it darts up a reed, each one was perfectly represented as I leisurely took up one after another from the pile and asked, 'What is the name of this? What does it do?'

I found that my visitor had lately received an order from a dealer at Yokohama to supply a complete set of birds for an English collector, for whom these were intended. I offered him, however, a reasonable price for the whole, which he willingly accepted, though he told me—what I quite believe—that he charged his Yokohama customer three times the price. I suspect that very few of these birds were shot; in fact, the collector told me that he captured the smaller species with bird-lime, and the larger, including the pheasants, with hair-springes. One characteristic bird was conspicuous by its absence. There were no cranes in the collection. Although five species are known as belonging to Japan, and three of them, the white-naped, white-headed, and especially the sacred crane, are frequently semi-domesticated in parks, public and private, and are familiar as continually recurring in Japanese art, yet I fear their fate in Japan in the near future is that of their congeners in England—extinction. I only once in the course of my rambles saw a flock of wild cranes —at least near enough to identify them—and this was in the Inland Sea, where a V-shaped party of the white-naped crane passed overhead. My friend, however, did not admit their extinction, but assured me he was far too loyal a subject of the Mikado and reverencer of the gods to commit the crime of molesting this sacred bird.

It must have been midnight before our ornithological *séance* came to an end—perhaps the most instructive natural-history lecture that I ever enjoyed. But all things come to an end, even a visit to Nikko, though we were loth to tear ourselves away from this fascinating spot and its surroundings. The final reckoning with our host was to me a most amusing illustration of the national courtesies. Mr. Kanaya acted as though the production of his bill were the most painful effort, and at length reluctantly he brought it forth, consisting of a number of Chinese scrawls on strips of tissue-paper. On bended knees and forehead touching the mat did my friend push it forward; I, bowing as well as my stiff Western back would permit me, placed the proper sum, wrapped in thin white paper, before him, for nothing is more ill-bred than to hand coin without its being wrapped in paper. Again it was received with bowing, low, lower, lowest; but it is always the rule of politeness to pay something more than the bill—in fact, to pay an hotel bill net would be considered an insult, or at least a mark of great dissatisfaction. Therefore, wrapping a yen (dollar) in white paper, I added it with low bows. It was returned with lower, and finally pressed upon the host with still more profound inclinations, and was at length duly and gratefully received. The bright little waiting-maid received her yen with the same show of modest reluctance.

CHAPTER IV

THE HAKONE LAKE

RETURNING from Nikko to Tokio was quitting the world of romance and ancient history to enter that of modern civilisation and fashion. We remained a few days under Bishop Bickersteth's hospitable roof, and diversified sight-seeing with much social intercourse, very Western in its character. We enjoyed parties official, ecclesiastical, and antiquarian, and under the happiest auspices made acquaintance with many charming cultured and literary residents of various nationalities. Not the least interesting was an evening with my old Palestine collaborator, General Palmer, R.E., now employed officially by the Japanese Government; and another evening with Dr. Whitney, the Secretary to the United States Legation, full of information, not only on Japanese history and politics, but also—which was to me a great boon—on the botany of the country. He supplied me with what proved invaluable in our subsequent rambles—a portable botanical press and a large supply of botanical paper, as well as a catalogue of the flora of Japan, in Japanese and Latin, to be the nucleus of my Japanese library. Before leaving Tokio, it was rather alarming to discover how truly we had verified the saying so far that the buying mania seizes everyone on landing, and never leaves them till they quit the shores. The packing of all our purchases, armour, swords, bronzes, birds, etc., and despatching them to Yokohama, was a good day's work.

And now we are on the rail again for a fifty miles' run to Kōzu. We had lovely peeps of Fuji San with her mantle of snow, recalling to me both in shape and situation the Peak of Teneriffe, which it very nearly equals in height. Fuji, indeed, for many days continued to be the central point round which our journeys revolved. From its immense height, so far excelling any other mountain in the central range, or backbone of Japan, from which it is separated by a wide extent of irregular plain, it gives from many points of view the impression of a mountain rising out of the sea in solitary state. No natural feature is so repeatedly depicted in the art of Japan, whether ceramic, pictorial, or poetic. The native appreciation of its central grandeur may be illustrated by an expression in a sermon of a young Japanese clergyman, that the verse, 'God so loved the world that He gave His only begotten Son' (John iii. 16), was the Fuji San of the Bible. Great and widespread was the consternation during the earthquake that occurred shortly after my visit, when the report was spread, and credited, that Fuji San had been destroyed. It was spoken of, not only as the greatest possible national loss, but as the most terrible omen for the future. Correspondingly great was the rejoicing when it was understood that the beloved and sacred mountain still raised her snowy peak heavenward, though a slight landslip had occurred on part of the slope.

The railway deposited us at Kōzu, where we had a short stroll on the beach, with a lovely view of the Bay of Odawara, and in the far distance the volcanic island of Enoshima, a reproduction of the Lipari Islands of the Mediterranean, and whose volcano is still as active as theirs. We then transferred ourselves to the tramcar which was to convey us to Yamoto, for, the traffic hardly promising to be remunerative enough for a railway, the Japanese, decidedly in advance of ourselves in these matters, at once laid down a tramline, while we are talking of light railways in aid of agriculture. We found the tramcars were divided into three classes, and, according to our usual custom, took second-class tickets. We were amused afterwards to find that the three omnibuses were identical in their appointments, and that the only distinction was that the first class preceded us by a few yards, and gave us the benefit of their dust, which we passed on, plus our own, to our more economical third-class followers. The road wound up a lovely valley, by the side of a turbulent torrent, and much resembled the drive to Balmoral by the Birks of Aberfeldy. Close to the starting-place at Odawara were the remains of what was once a very famous Daimio's castle, which was destroyed during the late revolution. From 1490 it was for more than a century the seat of government of the Shoguns of the Hōjō line. The name is preserved in a common Japanese proverb which applies to any purposeless chattering the expression, 'an Odawara Conference.' The phrase is said to have originated from the Hōjō chiefs, who had retired to their castle after a battle with the celebrated General Hideyoshi, spending some days in discussing the point whether it were better to attack the enemy, or to allow him to invest their stronghold. While they were unable to come to any conclusion, Hideyoshi solved the problem by a sudden onslaught, in which he stormed the fortress. Hence the proverb, an admirable illustration of the saying of our great general, 'Councils of war never fight.'

The tram runs parallel with the old Tōkaidō—*i.e.* the eastern sea-road—beautifully paved and macadamised with small pebbles, very narrow, and lined by grand old pines and cryptomerias, chiefly the former, forming an avenue of 380 miles between the capitals of the Mikado and the Shogun. It was, in fact, the great arterial line of the country, though now, with its wayside tea-houses, as deserted as our own great North Road. 'The old order changeth, and giveth place to new.'

Earlier writers on Japan, from the Dutch downwards, have given glowing pictures of the magnificence, the stir and bustle of the Tōkaidō of former times : of the Daimios in their ponderous palanquins, attended with their hundreds of henchmen, the two-sworded Samurai, resplendent in lacquered armour, as twice a year they made their leisurely procession to do homage to the Shogun. By the Tōkaidō all the inland commerce of the country was carried on packhorses; the whole line, we are told, was as crowded as the thoroughfares of a great city. Indeed, it must have been so, to judge by the countless tea-houses, many of them now deserted, which flank the avenue on either side. Public conveyances there were none, and as all travellers, except the few Daimios in their palanquins, made their journey on foot, and the Japanese travel very leisurely, the sleeping accommodation required must have been very great. One of the oldest English residents in Japan told us, at the Embassy, that he remembered before the revolution the processions of the Daimios along the Tōkaidō with their regiments of armed retainers, and how outrunners preceded them, compelling not only the common sort, but also Daimios of lesser degree, to stand out of the way as they passed. Even now the custom is still retained, not only on the road, but in Tokio and other towns, of outrunners on foot preceding the gentry, whether on horseback or in their carriages. Thus, but thirty years ago, one might have here beheld an exact reproduction of the spectacle of the feudal lords of Europe and their armed retainers.

Arrived at the tram terminus, Yamoto, we soon experienced the inconvenience of being on a foreigner-frequented track. We were still four miles from Miya-no-Shita, and we were encumbered with more than we could carry ourselves. The jinriksha men crowded round us like Arabs at Alexandria; though with the vociferations the likeness ends, for they were far too polite to seize our baggage, still less to drag us

WAYSIDE TEA-HOUSE.

by force to their own vehicles. We quietly sat down on the seat in front of the tea-house, assuming an air of perfect indifference as to whether we remained there for the day or not. We were assured it was impossible for us to walk. We smiled, and replenished our cups of green tea. On our asserting our firm intention of walking, the crowd looked at our baggage—a small portmanteau and two hold-alls—and assured us we could not carry it. 'We shall walk, and it may be carried,' we said, and more tea was sipped. 'It will take four jinrikshas,' they said. 'Two will be ample,' we replied. 'But these jinrikshas are not like the Tokio ones that you know,' they objected. We told them to go by the road, and we were going round by the mountain. 'That is impossible,' was the reply; 'the road is closed.' 'Then we will open it,' we answer, and are utterly unmoved by all arguments.

Seeing us calm and imperturbable, and not in the least hurried, two of them at length started with very easy loads by the road, and told us we should meet at the Naraya Hotel. We had a good travelling map, and felt no doubt as to our being able to find the way without a guide, although we had to cross a wooded mountain, round which the road makes a *détour*, and descend into the next valley, where we were certain to intersect the highway. It was fortunate that our further adventures were out of sight from Yamoto, for we missed the path, and after pulling ourselves through dense underwood of aucuba, deutzia, weigelia, and wisteria, up an almost perpendicular mountain, we found the scrub becoming really impenetrable, and were compelled after half an hour to retrace our steps to the main road. Our *amour-propre* would have been too sorely tried by the humiliation of going back to Yamoto to seek a guide; but we descended upon the next village, and soon found a man who knew the track, and who was willing to guide us. It was indeed a climb, even though we found the true route, but once arrived at the summit we were richly rewarded. We found ourselves on the crest of the ridge which forms the centre of the promontory province of Izu. Standing where we were, we could look down on either side into a deep mountain gorge, and following the ravine with our eye we could see where each opened into the Pacific Ocean on the right and the left of the mountain chain. Turning to the right, Fuji towered in front of us, her sides girdled with a cloud-belt; mountain ranges ran parallel on either side, affording a grand, though by no means overwhelming, panorama. We had now nothing to do but to follow the ridge westward until the path should rapidly descend to Miya-no-Shita. We dismissed our courteous guide, and walked for another hour and a half along the ridge, sometimes wooded and sometimes open. There were one or two marshy spots, the botany of which was quite novel to us, and we found some magnificent ladies' slipper (*Cypripedium japonicum*) in full blossom, with their enormous fan-shaped, flat leaves. It is very rare, and the queen of Japanese wildflowers, as is our species, though, alas! almost extinct, of the British flora. It is a curious coincidence that, as Sowerby a hundred years ago commenced his great work on British botany with an illustration of our ladies' slipper, so the illustrated history of the flora of Japan, begun, I believe, at an earlier date, and reaching to over a hundred volumes, of which the latter portion are only in manuscript, commences with a beautiful hand-coloured representation of this native species.

The sun was setting when we descended upon the road, a mile or two from Miya-no-Shita, and we soon reached our hotel, the Naraya, perched on a hillside amongst babbling hot streams and quaint artificial gardens. There was not much of the romantic within, though everything that could be desired for creature-comfort. Foreign furniture and fare at foreign prices are already established in this great health-resort—the Harrogate of Japan. We had just ordered dinner, when we were informed that a young Japanese gentleman requested an interview, or rather, as it was expressed, 'to hang on our honourable eyes.' With much ceremony he was ushered in, and with still more ceremony explained to us that he had espied the cypripedium protruding from my vasculum as we entered, and was anxious to know where we had found it, as he, too, was a botanist, and had been searching for it in vain for some days. For the information we gave him and for a specimen of the plant with root and bloom he overwhelmed us with gratitude. This, however, being one of the foreign hotels, it is patronised by very few natives, who generally, when visiting the springs, board at the many tea-houses in the villages round.

The next day was Sunday, and the second, and last, wet day I encountered during our rambles. We went up to the other foreign hotel, where we found a number of fellow-countrymen, and, thanks to the storm, had a fairly numerous company for Divine Service in the saloon. Thanks to the admirable postal arrangements of the country, we received a large batch of letters which had pursued us from place to place. The postal officials do not, as at home, disfigure the face of the letter or card by re-addressing it, but simply write the next address on a slip of tissue-paper, which is gummed at the edge and folded back over the missive. If it has again to be re-addressed, the same process is repeated, and thus I have a halfpenny post-card with eleven pages of address folded on to it, one after another, and which reached me at length without extra charge.

We spent a couple of days in exploring this lovely mountain glen. The charms of its position cannot be spoiled by all the efforts which enterprising hotel-keepers are making to Europeanise it. The constant appearance of English under the Chinese characters on the signboards of the shops, prevalent in Tokio and elsewhere, extends even to the villages. We came across some wonderful examples of 'English as she is spoke.' For instance, at the entrance to the grounds of the Naraya Hotel is the following notice: 'No trees and any flowers permitted to take off in this gardens. No fish permitted to catch in this ponds.' A man in the village has a horse to hire. On his signboard is a drawing of a man on horseback, and below simply the words, 'Lend horse.' On another board I read, *Fujinei Tei.* To let, the above-named tea-house, on the top of this hill. There mount Fuji on the up and island Enoshima on the down can be seen when weather is most splendidly. Leader, O-Niuga' (leader being Japanese English for owner or agent). Over a parcels delivery office near a station in Tokio was the following: 'Before station send at home and every state.'

After the rain the sun seemed rapidly to bring out the butterflies and to unfold the fern-fronds, the search for which gave zest to our rambles through these highland-like glens, affording continual change of landscape and partial peeps of Fuji San. But however many hours we wandered, the natural hot bath on our return would reinvigorate the most wearied. One noticed the change of colour each day, as the trees rushed out into foliage under the glowing sunshine, and the reeking moisture of the recent rainfall. One gentleman declared that he measured a young bamboo before going in to breakfast, and after breakfast. It had meanwhile reached another button of his waistcoat; and I quite believe him. My daughter, however, was inclined to suspect that he had changed his shoes for a thicker pair in the meantime!

No one can leave Miya-no-Shita with as little luggage as he entered it, for the village street is simply one long bazaar of open shops for the sale, not only of old armour, antiques, and photographs, but more especially of every kind of small wooden article, mostly inlaid, the manufacture of which is the industry of the districts, and which far surpass in finish, elegance, and ingenuity the choicest productions of Nice or Tunbridge Wells. They are all made from the different woods of the country, and at prices the modesty of which would shock the tradesmen of Switzerland. The winsome importunity and gracious address of those who sell them as you pass their booths are far more irresistible than the deafening advertisements and gesticulations of an Egyptian or Syrian bazaar.

But we must quit the luxuries of Miya-no-Shita if we would see the natural wonders and beauties of the mountain region around. With far less trouble than we should have had at home in a similar arrangement, after reducing our impedimenta to a hold-all apiece, a frame of botanical paper, and a satchel, all which could easily be carried by one man, we despatched our heavier luggage by two kuruma men to the nearest station, to be forwarded to Gotemba, which we hoped to reach in a few days, the men giving us a receipt, on the production of which we received our luggage some days after without the slightest difficulty.

Our first day's march was to the famous sacred village of Hakone, on the edge of a mountain lake, some eight miles distant over a mountain path, taking with us a man as porter and guide. However, he soon got so impatient at the time spent over plants and butterflies, which latter generally gave us the slip in the thick bush, that he declared he must

JAPANESE TRAVELLING CHAIR.

have double pay if we kept him back. As we were
not afraid now of losing our way, we let him go on.
We were reminded that Japan has already become
a hunting-ground of globe-trotters by meeting no
less than three parties of Englishmen, most of
whom were sensible enough to be pedestrians, though
three, who ought to have remained in Pall Mall,
were being carried down the hill in kagos, the native
sedan chair, a mode of conveyance that we felt was
only pardonable in the case of delicate ladies. The
hills on either side were bare and volcanic, and the
mass of dwarf bamboo through which our path lay
very monotonous. But every now and then, at a
turn in the track, a dainty little tea-house would
arrest us, and we could no more pass one without
expending a farthing on a cup of tea, than a toper
could resist a public at the corner. Ashi-no-Yu was
our halfway house, a village of bathing-houses and
native hotels for the hot sulphur springs. The
valley here reeked with sulphur smoke; the atmosphere was impregnated with it. There was not a
trace of vegetation, save the skeletons of trees, and
the spiræas, hydrangeas, and violets, which had
relieved the monotony of the bamboo thickets, had
all disappeared. We were not tempted to bathe
after what we saw of the publicity of the ablutions.
On the road beyond we passed a colossal Buddha in
an apse cut out of the basalt cliff; the figure, a very
beautiful one, is simply carved, along with the lotus-
flower on which the prophet sits, out of the native
rock, which has also been cut away behind it. It is

indeed a grand work, marvellously impressive on the lonely, desolate mountain-side. Rows of smaller Buddhas lined the short avenue to the shrine, but there is no temple or human habitation within sight.

There is an old tale connected with the little stream below, which may be worth repeating. A nobleman travelling by night let ten rin (equal to a halfpenny) drop out of his tinder-case into the water, and then spent fifty rin in torches to recover the lost piece of money. When his friends laughed at him for spending five times as much to recover what he had lost, he retorted : 'Gentlemen, you are very foolish, and do not understand political economy. You have no feeling of benevolence. If I had not searched for the ten-rin piece, it would have been for ever lost, sunk at the bottom of the stream. Now, the fifty rin which I have spent on torches will remain in circulation among the tradesmen. It is no matter whether they, or I, or some one else has them, but not a single one of this sixty rin has been lost, and this is a clear gain to the nation.' We see that political economy—whether it be in accordance with Adam Smith or not, I do not say— is no new science to Japan.

Soon after passing the image and stream we had our first glimpse of the mountain lake and the picturesque Hakone village at its head, with a fine cryptomeria avenue for the last mile of the way. The hotel proved to be a Japanese house attempting to ape English ways, and with English prices spoilt by tourists. However, we had a pleasant airy room and wide balcony for the daytime, with the finest of mat floors, divided into three by paper walls for our bedrooms, the beds being made on the floor. Native so-called beds—that is, the soft, clean mat, and futon, or wadded quilt—are most welcome after a hard day's walk, but on native wood pillows I never could rest my head. To attempt it suggested instantaneously the thought of King Charles on the block, with the head ready to roll off on the other side.

I fear I shall sink in the estimation of those of my readers for whom conchology has no charms when I confess that our first expedition was a stroll along the edge of the lake in search of freshwater shells among the scanty patches of reeds which occasionally fringe it, and amongst which we waded in black mud. I was stimulated to this by one of the young Englishmen whom we had met in the morning, who assured me he had found on the beach of the lake a freshwater shell identical with the Melania of the Sea of Galilee. We succeeded in collecting various species, amongst them the one alluded to, but found, as one often does, that similarity is not identity. We returned in time to watch the evening sun from our balcony, which soon set behind Fuji. The effect was grand, for the sky was cloudless; and though Fuji must yield the palm to the Peak of Teneriffe, I never there saw finer sunset colouring. We saw it white, rosy blush, pink, and finally, just at sunset, the snowclad mountain, with the sun exactly behind it, looked deep black in a pale golden setting.

The Hakone lake is, so far as we can learn, of unknown depth. It is, in fact, an enormous mountain tarn over 5,000 feet above the sea-level. It is curious that, with the exception of one very small outlet at the north end, there are no streams from it. On the plain below are few or no natural streams, and it is said that many centuries ago the mountain wall was tunnelled by manual labour, and the upper waters tapped, and from the rocky sluices flows a flood sufficient to irrigate millions of acres of the Suruga province ; and this enables the inhabitants to raise the vast quantities of rice on which the country is dependent for its very existence. Water, and a sufficient supply of it to immerse the fields either at once or in compartments, is the first necessity of the rice-farmer. As rice must be sown, transplanted, and grown under water, immense areas of irrigated fields are necessary. A proof of the very early civilisation of Japan is found in the stupendous tunnels and the dams by which the mountain streams have been blocked for the purpose of irrigating the lower plains, and by which the noisy, foaming torrents have been changed into silent and useful, if unromantic, servants. These huge reservoirs are tapped when required, and conveyed, often for miles, along artificial canals or ditches, each field securing a supply as the stream passes, by little locks ; whilst in the lower plains treadwheels are used to pump the water on to each compartment. All this is regulated by law most rigidly enforced. To steal a neighbour's water was formerly a capital offence.

THE HAKONE LAKE, FIVE THOUSAND FEET ABOVE SEA-LEVEL.

Just on the right hand of our hotel a little peninsula runs out into the lake, on which is a modest though extensive building, one of the country palaces of the emperor, and which he generally visits for a fortnight in summer. The grounds had only recently been laid out, and their beauty was future, not present. However, unlike the Egyptian Khedive, the Mikado of Japan refuses to waste his subjects' money on imperial residences. Thus he declined, shortly after the beginning of the present war, to have a palace built for his reception at Hiroshima. By his refusal he intensified the enthusiastic loyalty of his people.

From our lake dwelling at Hakone, for such in the full sense our pile-supported châlet was, we made an early start to the other end of the lake, a row of about six miles, with Fuji in front the whole way. The scenery of the upper end of the lake was much bolder than at the lower, the pine forest coming down to the water's edge, many of the peeps recalling Derwentwater. Our goal was Gotemba, a little town from which we planned to explore Fuji and its neighbourhood, and we took with us a Hakone man with a long bamboo to carry our baggage. We stepped on shore from our boat, prepared for a twenty miles' mountain walk, with a delightful sense of independence.

As we wound up the narrow path we very soon lost all traces of forest, and rapidly reached a succession of rolling downs, bare and desolate but for a few unwholesome-looking tufts of rush. We were here quite out of the usual tourists' beat, and at a teahouse at the top of the first bare ridge—for whatever else there is not, there is everywhere a tea-house—we prudently provisioned ourselves for the day with two parcels of cold boiled rice, and half a dozen hardboiled eggs. After passing through some weary bamboo scrub we reached Ubago, a collection of hotels and hot sulphur water baths, and the whole air saturated with sulphur. The baths are long buildings of one storey round squares, with the steaming baths open in front, each tenanted by naked bathers of both sexes sitting promiscuously in the hot water, open to all passers-by. In this respect there is certainly a want of decency in Japan, but it is, so far as I saw, an exception; for, taken on the whole, there is less to be seen that offends one's sense of delicacy and propriety in Japan than in any other Eastern country I have visited.

After resting for a quarter of an hour on a mat, of course sipping green tea, we started up a steep path, through forest with an undergrowth of sweet-scented white dwarf daphne, which perfumed the surrounding atmosphere. There was also a dwarf pyrus, with brilliant red bloom; quantities of an orchid, promising to be a gigantic cypripedium, but which does not flower till July, and various other to us botanic novelties. Crossing the next ridge, we found ourselves in a steep desolate valley, with ash-heap, sulphur hillocks, steam holes, and roaring boiling water tumbling under the crust upon which we trod, altogether a weird scene of desolation, for here there

OJIGOKU, OR GREAT BOILING SPRING.

are no sulphur plants like those which characterise the similar sulphuric springs and deposits of Callirrhoe in the land of Moab. It is called Ojigoku, or the Great Hell, but was named last year, in honour of the emperor's visit, Owa kidani, or the valley of the great boiling. Both names are well-earned. It was a splendid opportunity for investigating volcanic phenomena on a small scale, but we were repeatedly cautioned by our guide to beware where we trod, as more than one traveller have lost their lives through the edges of the thin crust, which is cracked in every direction, and sometimes has wide fissures.

We reached another crest, and lo, a complete transformation scene. In place of the sulphurous desolation and mephitic steam, we found an almost obliterated track, under thickets of deutzia, azalea, and other flowering shrubs of every colour, the azaleas predominating. The flora of this neighbourhood is in many respects very peculiar, containing many plants which we never found elsewhere. Another crest to cross, and we had to brush through bamboo brake, and across a flat valley for three miles, highly cultivated and studded with villages, till we faced a wooded and apparently perpendicular mountain.

How were we to get up? 'There,' replies our coolie, as he rests the pole with his burden cleverly balanced on his long bamboo alpenstock. 'Not promising,' and we looked at each other, and zigzagged up the side by a series of sloping notches cut in the cliff. However, when we at length reached the summit of the Otomi Toge Pass we were rewarded for all our scramble. Standing on the ridge we could, at the same moment, look over the plain we had crossed an hour before into the lake shining at its further end, and on the other side over the range, the vast plain through which the Tōkaidō runs, stretching unbroken to the slopes of Fuji, which stood out in undimmed splendour without a cloud, his snow gilded by the afternoon sun. Straight ahead were the snow-capped granite peaks of the provinces of Hida and Echu. The plain, thick with villages, coppices, fields, avenues, and trees of all sorts, looked more like Kent or Surrey than Japan as I had yet seen it. And this impression of its English character was soon intensified when, gaily tripping down the mountain side, my daughter said she had never before trod on turf all the years she had been in Japan. We were delighted with the tall, pale, purple daisy—at least it seemed to me a true *Bellis*, but, if not, was certainly an aster very like it, met with by us here for the first time, and which covers the whole meadow-like slopes.

This was the first district I had found where sheep might be reared, for there is no dwarf bamboo, as there is everywhere else, a plant which is fatal to pasturing sheep, and which is a simple explanation of their absence in the country. At the little tea-house on the top where we were glad to rest, we met several fellow-countrymen who had come in the other direction with kagos or chairs, and who did not exchange salutations with mere pedestrians. I took the opportunity of skinning a curious little black shrew mouse with a bushy tail which I had obtained in the bamboo brake. When we had reached the bottom of the range, we were rather disappointed to find that we had still more than four miles to walk; yet who could be tired as we trod those narrow Devonshire lanes, ceaselessly using our butterfly-net under the long hedges of camellia, the falling crimson blooms of which absolutely smothered the smooth path which they overhung? In fact, here the camellia took the place of the hawthorn, and the azaleas of the apple trees of Southern England. At length we came upon Gotemba, which is one long street, along which we trudged for more than a mile before we found quarters at a thoroughly native inn, exquisitely clean as usual, but without a solitary chair or table. We inquired their charges, and after a little bargaining closed for a yen and a half, or five shillings, a day for the two of us, including three native meals, as well as apartments and attendance. On asking for a hot bath, I was ushered to one in the large kitchen, in which a man was already stewing, and created much surprise by my fastidiousness in declining to share the bath with him, though I was assured there was room for two in it!

Eleven hours on foot made us thoroughly appreciate our couches, though they were only the mat-flooring, with futons under and over us, and others rolled up for a pillow. We slept well in spite of the noises, for the hotel was extensive, and there was only a sliding paper wall between the rooms, while visitors seemed to be coming and going throughout the night. I was aroused during my first sleep by

the visit of a policeman, who, having heard that
foreigners had arrived, hurriedly came to examine
our passport, and insisted upon seeing my daughter,
from whom he wanted explanations as to how or why
we had such an unusually extensive one. When his
curiosity and scruples were satisfied, he was of course
effusive in his politeness. His visit reminded me of
two things which I have often observed in Japan—
their absolute indifference to times and seasons, and
the amusing self-importance of the little officials, far
superior to Bumbledom at home. If a message has
to be delivered, whether unimportant or not, the
time of day matters not. If the mail has arrived and
the postman is up, he will rouse you to deliver letters
at 2 A.M., especially if one of them is registered and
must be receipted with ink, and you happen to have
no ink in your bedroom. In red tape they surpass
France and equal Russia. A friend of mine was
travelling with a passport which authorised him to
visit certain places in a particular order. He wished
to vary this order, which had been filled in without
his being consulted, but was informed in a certain
town that he must go west rather than east, as he
wished. Expostulation was in vain, but after waiting
a few days, when the officials saw he was an awkward
customer who intended to hold firm, they informed
him, that though it was their duty to compel him to
leave the city by the west road, yet after pursuing
it for a mile or two he would find a cross-country
path which would take him in the other direction.
As an instance of the Japanese love of keeping to

the letter of the law, the following may be quoted. A certain bridge was found unsafe for heavy traffic, though still available as a foot-bridge, and a notice was accordingly posted, 'No animals allowed to cross this bridge.' After a time a formal complaint was made that it was impossible to insist on this order being obeyed, for rats would still continue to cross. A solemn conclave was held, at which it was decided that it was impossible to prevent the rats having their free course, and yet that disobedience to an official edict was not to be tolerated, and therefore the wording of the notice was altered to run, 'No large animal allowed to cross this bridge.' Even then the malcontents were not quite satisfied, for where was the line to be drawn between large and small animals?

At Gotemba, as at all Japanese inns, the bill of fare varies not for breakfast, dinner, and supper. We had fish soup in a little lacquer basin, the floating bits of fish having to be caught with chopsticks— to a raw hand like myself quite as serious an affair as the original capture in the stream. Perhaps another kind of soup, made with seaweed, vegetables, or dried fish, might come instead. There were green pickles in a lacquer saucer; raw eggs, probably having been kept long enough to have a flavour, a fresh egg being considered very insipid. When near the coast we should have had varieties of shell-fish, sea-urchins, and half-cooked octopus, or sea-fish. But here these were represented by delicious mountain trout, nicely baked. To such condiments at a wedding-feast or at the new year would be added a lobster, emblematic of long life, with the wish, 'May you live to such an age that your back is as bent as a lobster's!' All these are served to each person on a small square lacquer tray, with feet a few inches high. In front of us was always placed a small wooden tub with a lid, filled with steaming rice, and served with a flat wooden ladle, not unlike a painter's spatula, with which each from time to time refilled at pleasure the little rice bowl. As all the dishes are served on the little trays at once, the chief duty of the waitress is to keep the rice-bowl supplied; in fact, rice is the substitute not only for bread, but practically for all our food save meat and vegetables.

There are no sweets at the regular meals, but green tea always follows, and, if specially ordered, *saké*, served hot in a long-necked porcelain flask. This *saké* is prepared from rice malt with very little hops, and resembles much the heavy muddy beer of an inferior country public-house. Cold, it is certainly not palatable, and when hot only tolerable to my taste.

More difficult than the management of chopsticks, at which I soon became a tolerable adept, was the sitting on the floor to eat, and I never during my sojourn succeeded in—I will not say gracefully, but even in any way with ease or comfort—accommodating myself to the native habits in this respect, and soon began to feel that a room furnished with but one chair and table was a luxurious one. If I rolled up a futon and sat on it my tray was far below me, and either a more supple back or chop-

PILGRIM GOING UP FUJILAMA.

sticks of abnormal length were needed; or if I reversed the order of things and mounted my dinner tray on this temporary seat, what was I to do on the floor with my aching legs, that refused to be tucked under me, as those of my little Japanese friends have learned to be from babyhood?

Though the ascent of Fuji at this early season of the year was impossible, we determined to reach the forest which covers its lower slopes and penetrate as far as the snow would permit us. We made an early start for the foot of the mountain in jinrikshas, or, as they are more properly in Japan called, kurumas, zigzagging for several miles through narrow lanes with camellia hedges laden with bloom. At length we emerged from this Kentish scenery into paddy fields, crossing countless little brooks, fed by the mountain snow, hardly deep enough to be called dells, but the sides of which were clad with overhanging azaleas, red, white, yellow, purple, and pink, and many other choice shrubs, while the black water ousel, the representative of the familiar dipper of our northern streams, darted up and down the brook, or briskly jerked his tail as he lighted on a stone in the water. The farmers were busy preparing the fields for planting out the rice. Rice-growing is toil indeed, and has passed into a Japanese proverb for hard or weary labour. Men were wading knee-deep in the black mud, leading horses or oxen attached to a long rake, which does duty for a plough, and pounds the soaked clods until the whole becomes reduced to the consistency of pea soup, and is then ready for the young plants. Ascending from the rice fields, the road and soil were alike formed of black volcanic ash like a Durham pit-heap.

Arrived at Subashiri, the last village before the ascent, we found the place *en fête*, and had the opportunity of seeing at our leisure the humours of a Japanese country fair.

The village is a long one, over half a mile, and at the upper end terminates in a Shinto temple, embowered in dense cryptomeria grove and avenue. The main street is wide, and planted with flowering trees on both sides. Between these, bamboo tops with their feathery foliage had been set all along, fastened with long lines of twine, and covered like a Christmas-tree with bits of red and white paper. All the women and children were in their bright holiday dresses; the streets were lined with the stalls of vendors of all kinds of goods, from large mats to dolls' clothes. Cheapjacks were advertising their wares; some strolling players had a platform mounted on rollers, and were performing free gratis; on a more elevated stage pretty dancing girls were performing a Japanese opera and ballet combined; crowds of country folk, with bales of rice straw and mats, as well as all kinds of farm produce to sell, combined business with pleasure. There were penny peeps for one rin (one-tenth of a halfpenny); a grand model of Fuji on a barrow; Punch whacking Judy exactly as he does elsewhere, and Toby by his side. There were more horses assembled than I had yet seen in Japan. It was indeed the village feast of the olden time, with all the quaint Japanese surroundings. Paper lanterns lined the avenue to the temple preparatory for a great illumination at night. Here we found a grand service proceeding. The Shinto priests vest and revest in public, and continually change their coloured stoles. There was an empty shrine, with the two long strips of cut white paper hanging in front. The ritual was very moderate, but we were unable to understand the chantings and recitations of which the service, performed by the priests alone, consisted.

At lunch in the village inn fresh mountain trout and egg soup were welcome delicacies, and in consideration for our foreign weakness our hostess found two chairs, which were indeed appreciated. From the village in the afternoon we wandered on over volcanic ashes through a thin wood, and then for two hours mounted through the forest. I got near the edge of the snow-line, or at least to the snow lying under the pine trees as yet untouched by the spring sun, and in a small open space in the middle of the forest, filled with flowering shrubs and entirely secluded, had a splendid opportunity for watching some of the rarest birds of Japan and noting their habits. It seemed to be the rendezvous of song-birds, as I sat completely concealed by the foliage of an evergreen shrub. The beautiful narcissus flycatcher took its perch on a twig within a yard of my head; the Siberian blue-tail, and, best of all, the lovely Japanese waxwing, fearlessly hopped about in pursuit of the small butterflies; the Siberian

M

blackbird with its white belly, and the black and white ousel (*Merula cardis*) perched at the opposite end of the opening, entered as competitors in a singing match, while many a warbler whistled and titmouse chirped unseen. It was an hour's ornithological education such as I have rarely had, and though I was not able to pay my respects to the Lady of Fuji in her crater at the summit, as every pilgrim ought, I was amply rewarded by the fruits of my pilgrimage.

It is interesting to note that as we have retained the ancient British names of our rivers and of many of our hills, so the name of Fuji has no meaning in the vernacular, but is kindred to the Ainu word for fire mountain, handed down from the time when the aboriginal Ainu inhabited the land. It is held to be the residence of a goddess, Fuji-sen-gen, and is, therefore, a sacred mountain and place of pilgrimage. The legend says that Fuji arose in a night, and that at the same time Lake Biwa was hollowed out, and tradition adds that this was about the year 330 B.C. There are historic records of eruptions from 799 A.D., and the last of any importance was in 1707 A.D., when the hump on the south side of the mountain was formed. In this eruption Tokio itself was covered with six inches of ashes. At present the only sign of activity is a little steam and smoke from cracks close to the crater on the side facing Subashiri. We only ascended about 4000 feet, but the forest and thicket extend 3000 feet higher.

As an illustration of the quickness and imitative

powers of the people, I may mention an incident of this day's ramble. I had been followed to the forest by two men, who always kept me in view. It seems that one of them had learned from our kuruma men that we had been butterfly-hunting. They had followed our example, but were too shy to accost us, though they told our men. When invited, they summoned courage at last to come to me, and offered me about a dozen butterflies which they had caught, and folded in triangular bits of paper, exactly as I had done. They gracefully offered me the fruits of their chase, and when I accepted and thanked them, giving them a two-sen piece, they beamed with delight, and we each bowed to the ground. The men evidently enjoyed the pleasure of gratifying a stranger.

Another instance of graceful courtesy. At a little farmhouse, as we were returning in the evening, the blaze of azaleas and the neatness of a garden arrested us for a moment. As we stopped to admire, an old woman came out and insisted on filling my daughter's arms with gorgeous branches of bloom. She reciprocated by handing a picture-card and a tract, and we discovered that the woman was a Christian, and cousin of one of our kuruma men.

CHAPTER V

NAGOYA

THE next day we took the train from Gotemba to Nagoya, 176 miles further on, and the fourth city of Japan in population, 350,000, a principal seat of the porcelain manufacture. Here the Canadian branch of our Church has a mission, supported by Wyclif College, Toronto. The journey was accomplished in eight hours, through a rich, fertile plain, the most extensive in the country, thickly peopled and well-wooded. Part of our route lay close to the sea, and we crossed the mouths of two rivers, wide and shallow, by trestle bridges, each nearly a mile long. We had among our fellow-passengers Bishop Bickersteth, who was going on beyond us. We had also in our carriage a native lady of very winning and refined appearance, who soon introduced herself to my daughter as a Christian from Osaka. Three officers also entered the carriage, one of whom, a very gentlemanly man, the head of the police at Nagoya, spoke English, and told me he knew our missionaries there. He told me he felt very much complimented by finding that I smoked the light tobacco of the country, which, he said, most foreigners despised. At a roadside station luncheon boxes were purchased. For ten sen, that is fivepence, I had handed to me a beautifully-made oblong chip box with a lid, full of rice; a pair of new wooden chop-sticks, still joined at one end, to show they had never been used, in a pretty paper envelope; and another similar box, done up in picturesque paper, containing nine different articles of food, arranged like a bouquet, with strips of green bamboo leaf, cut with scissors, to separate them. It was a perfect gem of Japanese art and neatness. Among the items were a very small boiled cuttle-fish, which was very good, white beans cooked with sugar, boiled seaweed, pickle, a mushroom, a tiny rice-flour pudding, a rice-flour sponge cake, a lump of Turkish delight, and two vegetables, to me unknown. It is needless to say that the dishes were microscopical, and were not very much larger than the dolls' feasts to which grandchildren invite me. We had a kuruma ride of two miles through the vast city from the station of Nagoya to the hospitable roof of our Canadian friends, the Rev. J. C. and Mrs. Robinson.

Nagoya is full of interest, ancient and modern, historical and artistic. The central feature, which catches the eye from every part of the city, is the castle, probably the finest specimen of an old Daimio's residence in the country, and as now it is government property, it is one of the few that has been carefully preserved. It is the Alnwick Castle of Japan, and was held by the first peer of the realm next to the Shogun. The founder of the house was the son of Iyeyasu. The castle was built in 1610; the outer enceinte is very extensive, and is occupied by the garrison, but the central citadel and donjon-keep are indeed a marvellous wooden pile, and a grand specimen of barbaric splendour.

A moat, still full of water, surrounds the outer wall, formed of mighty cyclopean masonry, all the walls sloping and slightly curving outwards. Then there is a wide open space with gardens, orchards, and fields, and here are the extensive barracks and parade ground, where formerly were the quarters of the prince's Samurai and the offices of the province. Within this is an inner moat, now dry, and inhabited by a small herd of deer, and above it rises another cyclopean wall, surmounted by wooden battlements.

The centre keep, a massive structure of five stories supported by stone walls, but within entirely wooden, is surrounded by a bewildering number of apartments, of one or two stories, of which, alas! the furniture has all disappeared, though the exquisitely carved and gilded ceilings and the partitioned panels of each chamber are decorated with very fine paintings, as are the alcoves and the wooden doors between the different sets of apartments. Each room is generally devoted to a distinct subject painted in panels. Thus we have the history of the tiger in one room, in another of the leopard, in another pheasants, of which five different species are admirably depicted; deer, hawks, squirrels, woodpeckers, etc., etc., have all their separate apartments. Others are devoted to ancient Japanese life, civil and military. In one, all their games are beautifully painted in a series of twelve; in another a painting of horse-racing occupies a whole side, and among the spectators stand two

NAGOYA CASTLE

unmistakable Dutchmen. In another a tournament is depicted, where a Japanese lady is evidently the queen of beauty. Another, the richest apartment of the whole—the one kept for the use of the Shogun when he should visit the prince—is decorated with fancy Chinese scenery, while in the alcove are powerful carvings of cranes, tortoises and cocks, the latter perched on a drum. In one of the bird panels in another room is a hole cut out exactly the shape of a swallow, the myth being that the painter made so perfect a swallow that it flew away in the night and left its place vacant!

At the bottom of the keep is a very deep and inexhaustible well. It is difficult to describe the massive piles of wood employed in this huge structure. The boards of the corridors are so arranged that it is impossible to walk on them without their creaking, and so warning is given of any one's approach. Each storey is roofed with sheets of copper, and it is said the fortress could accommodate 25,000 defenders. From the top of it we had a magnificent view of the vast plain, using our glasses to some purpose.

The angles of the roof of the summit are ornamented by two golden dolphins gleaming in the sunlight, and catching the eye from every part of the city. One of these was sent to the Vienna Exhibition in 1873, and was wrecked on its way back, but with great difficulty recovered from the sea, and restored to its height, whence it is never to descend again. But there is a tale of a thief who took advantage of a stormy night to fly a kite over one of them, and thus attempted to get the gold plating, but was caught and boiled in oil for his pains, after which the flying of large kites was prohibited in the province. The dolphins are eight feet and a half in height, and are said to be worth £40,000.

The historic castle is not the only attraction of Nagoya, which well deserves more time than the three days we were able to bestow upon it. A bright avenue of blossoming cherry trees leads up to the Buddhist temple called Higashi Hongwanji, which is remarkable not only for its external beauty and its internal splendour, but as being one of the very few fine religious buildings erected in the present century, and which rivals if it does not surpass the structures of ancient art. It is the cathedral of the Hongwanji sect, or reformed Buddhists, a sect not more than 300 years old, who desire to restore their religion to what they believe was its primitive purity. Their leading tenet, which distinguishes them from the numerous other subdivisions of Buddhism in Japan, is the doctrine of justification by faith, that is, they teach that if your good works and penances are not of themselves sufficient to insure your rapid attainment of Nirvana, or absorption into the infinite, the desired end may be attained by faith in the Amida incarnation of Buddha. As this sect embraces the most thoughtful and intellectual part of the population, the prominence that it gives to the doctrine of justification by faith removes one great obstacle to the reception of Christianity, if it even does not pave the way for it.

A careful survey of this temple affords sufficient evidence that neither art nor taste have degenerated in the country; though there are no signs of any development or originality. But can we say more, or as much, of architectural art in our own country? Where is the trace of originality in any one of our modern architects? Have our Gilbert Scotts or Butterfields done any more than simply reproduce the older designs; or are their most original works anything more than the taking to pieces, after the manner of a Chinese puzzle, the masterpieces of our old designers, and reproducing them in a somewhat varied arrangement? This temple, which is 120 feet long, is divided into a nave and two aisles, with a deep chancel and a central gilt shrine, with an image of Buddha on a platform, enriched with exquisitely designed carvings and sculpture in wood, painted and gilded. The shrine at the termination of one of the aisles contains a portrait of the founder of the sect. On both sides of the central image are several gilt screens, on which are very cleverly painted landscapes. But what struck me most in this temple was the number and wonderful variety of fabulous and supernatural beings—in fact, a repertory of all that is mythological and legendary in the fairy tales of old Japan. The heroes of romance or of fairy tales are represented riding on fish, tortoises, cranes, frogs, and dragons. All the figures I believe can be explained by references to the old Japanese mythology, of which on these points at least I must confess my ignorance.

One other small temple is well worth a visit

for the extraordinary collection of images which it contains. On both sides of and behind the shrine are galleries, where are arranged on stages one above another small statues of the five hundred original disciples of Buddha. Each one of the five hundred is different, both in face and costume. No two can be found alike. The work is said to be about three hundred years old. What strikes the visitor most is that there is nothing conventional about them, nothing of the inanimate uniformity of the Buddhas, but all are full of expression. The artists must have indeed been geniuses to devise the different faces, all of which they could not have had before them. In fact, they seem quite to have understood the characteristic types of the various peoples of the East. Some are admirable Hindu types, others Mongolian, Chinese, and Malay, besides the ordinary Japanese. There is every variety too of individual expression. Some are grave and dignified, others haughty and imperious, some smiling, others with an amusing Pharisaic expression of self-satisfaction. Their attitudes are as various as their countenances, standing, kneeling, recumbent, praying, blessing, or riding on horses, elephants, etc. The verger assured us that every one who searches can find his own likeness among these Rakan.

We had intended to leave Nagoya earlier than we did, but we missed our train owing to it starting by the station clock, which was fast. On our remonstrating with the officials they were most profuse in apologies, and would be delighted to put

TEMPLE AT NAGOYA, CONTAINING FIVE HUNDRED IMAGES

the clock to any time we wished. They at once put it back ten minutes to oblige us, but this did not recall our train. However, we were able well to utilise the extra time. We gave a day to visiting the porcelain manufactories of Nagoya, under the guidance of a highly educated, intelligent Japanese Christian gentleman. Nagoya is a great manufacturing centre for every kind of porcelain, not only for that which bears its name, but also for the modern Satsuma and cloisonné wares. We saw the whole processes, from the mixing of the clay, the modelling, painting, and baking, to the final glazing. Much of it was very like the operations which I have seen in Worcester, though much less depended on machinery, and more on the accuracy of the individual hand and eye. This was especially the case with the painting. All Nagoya ware is hand-painted, and we watched for a long time an old man sitting on the ground, with an unbaked vase between his legs, which he was covering with artistic designs with great rapidity, and no copy before him. He rapidly finished his work, and having passed it on, took another vase, which he would decorate quite in another style, again without a copy. Having passed this on, he would take its fellow and reproduce exactly the same pattern without once referring to the other, simply from memory. It seemed to make no difference whether the subject were landscape, a garden scene, birds, or human figures, all were performed with equal accuracy and rapidity. This skill is acquired by long training and practice. These decorators of the ceramic art, like the other artists of their country, never copy Nature, but study the recognised masterpieces of the artists of the olden time, whose works they reproduce over and over again with Chinese accuracy, even to the minutest touches, never venturing beyond the original.

And so in landscape art. No Japanese will attempt, for instance, to sketch Fuji from Nature, still less to attempt a subject not selected by the old masters. There are, perhaps, about fifty such scenes, which have the same place in art as the Madonnas of Raphael and Murillo in Europe, and these are well known to every educated Japanese, who would think it a profanation to attempt a sketch of a scene not included in the classical selection. We followed the vases from the artist to the kiln, the delicate manipulation of which showed how much depends upon a practised eye and touch; and then finally to the glazing oven. We had the satisfaction of including among our subsequent purchases a pair of vases of which we had watched the whole process of manufacture.

Another department of this large factory was devoted to the manufacture of modern Satsuma ware, the distinctive characteristic of which seems to be a peculiar minute reticulated cracking beneath the glaze. The art of this manufacture has only lately been resuscitated, in consequence of the immense prices obtained for the old extinct Satsuma ware. So far as I could detect the process, this peculiar effect is produced in the baking, perhaps by its being taken out and immersed in some liquid or exposed to a sudden change of temperature before the process is completed. Probably we were not shown everything, as it is not likely that what must be almost if not altogether a secret should be revealed to strangers.

But we did watch with much interest the cloisonné manufacture, which is again an example of the marvellous memory and imitative power of Japanese artistic workmen. The vase to be operated upon was slightly dried rather than baked before it came into the artist's hands. He was supplied with long rolls of metal slips or flattened wire about the width of a watch-spring, say the eighth of an inch, which looked like nickel, but which were, I believe, copper. In fact, had it not been for their colour, I should have taken them for watch springs. These, with marvellous delicacy, the workman twisted into the desired shape, and pressed lightly into the soft clay, snipping them when required with a pair of pliers, and forming the outline of leaves or birds, or whatever else he desired to represent.

When his pattern was thus completed, he filled the various interstices of this network from a palette by his side, on which were arranged little piles of paste of various colours. There might be from a dozen to twenty pastes of different shades employed for a single vase.

The patterns of some of the borders were extremely small, some of the loops being but the fortieth part of an inch across. For these he twisted his wire with minute pliers. This part of the work was really almost microscopic, and yet done with the accuracy of a machine. When these tiny partitions had received a portion of the metallic paste, the ware was taken to the kiln, slightly baked and then refilled. This process is repeated several times, when the article is smoothed down and polished by another artist. A most costly kind of cloisonné ware is formed on copper instead of porcelain. This manufacture, however, did not come under our notice.

Having completed the pattern according to his taste, he then roughed the field not occupied by his design with a wooden instrument, when the vase was ready for the first kiln and then for the polisher. After spending half a day in inspecting the manufacture, we visited the show-room, which would have done credit to Regent Street, and five boxes told the tale of the spoil that had become ours. We had no further trouble with our purchases, which were sent on by the vender to Osaka, and thence to England, where they arrived without a single fracture. The packing of china is an art in Japan. Every article is packed separately in rice straw twisted tightly round the article, and the ends ingeniously tucked in, so that each piece of porcelain looks like a hard straw ball, and can be let fall without fracture.

We afterwards visited in the company of our Japanese friend, who was a well-known connoisseur in art, a great sale of furniture, lacquer and bronze, the property of the son of a celebrated Daimio, who had been ruining himself on the turf at Paris, and was compelled to raise money by the sale of the family heirlooms. These were displayed in the upper storey of the principal hotel in the place. All the partitions having been removed, the whole formed one spacious gallery, along the sides and down the centre of which the various articles were arranged, each having a strip of tissue paper attached to it with the price distinctly marked in Japanese characters. Thus there was no bargaining, no abatement, no competition. The visitor simply told the salesman the number of the article he wished for, and it was handed to him. There were many ancestral relics of great intrinsic value, very fine bronzes at a figure quite beyond my limits; but guided by our Japanese friend we spent a few pounds in antique lacquer ware inlaid with mother of pearl, which we found afterwards was considered a great bargain. Amongst others a tray of ancient Corean lacquer, the manufacture of which is quite different from the Japanese, and is now a lost art.

On Sunday morning we had a walk of two miles to the house used as a church, which is simply an ordinary house in a busy street. Passing through the outer apartment, all took off their shoes. The next room was the vestry, and beyond it the church, consisting of three rooms thrown into one, with the communion table at the further end, where the paper walls had been removed, so that the church opened on the pretty little garden behind. The congregation consisted of rather less than thirty adults, and a Sunday-school of about a dozen children. Chairs were found for Mrs. Robinson and myself, but everyone else sat on the floor, while the bishop in full robes officiated in stocking feet. We began with the Confirmation Service. Six converts were confirmed, one of them a leading lawyer, another a man of education, who was to be a catechist. The bishop gave the address before the service, and Holy Communion followed, of course all in Japanese, which, though I could not understand, yet was able to follow, an advantage of a liturgy that I have often felt in foreign lands. It was an intensely interesting spectacle, and recalled in imagination the infant churches in the Acts of the Apostles. The occasion when St. Paul received into the church Dionysius the Areopagite and the lady Damaris could not have been very different in its surroundings. There were various other services and schools in the afternoon and evening, for neither the bishop nor any other of the missionaries spare themselves, but I remained at home.

We left Nagoya and its 125,000 inhabitants reluctantly. We could well have spent more time there with our charming hosts, who are specimens of earnest missionaries, and an honour to the Canadian Church.

Our next stage was Gifu, a town of 40,000 inhabitants, the capital of the province of Mino, and the employment of whose people is the manufacture of paper lanterns; the rearing of silkworms; and in summer the fishing with cormorants, which is really the important industry of the place, and which attracts many spectators.

This art, like falconry, is of great antiquity, and like it, has been derived from China. Old Willoughby, more than two hundred years ago, described this mode of fishing with cormorants as it had been carried on in old England long before his time, and refers to several authorities, as J. Faber and Mendoza. In England, however, it had become extinct, until recently it was resuscitated by that well-known falconer Captain F. Salvin. It would seem that the sport was introduced into Europe in the beginning of the 17th century by the Dutch, from whose country it spread to France and England, and was a favourite amusement of both James I. and Charles I. Probably it was from Japan rather than China that the earlier voyagers derived their knowledge of this mode of fishing. Cormorant fishing, as I have seen it carried on on a large scale in the Chinese province of Che-Kiang in no way differs from the Japanese method. The cormorants, which are taken very young, are taught to feed from the hand, and then allowed to fish for themselves with a long string attached to their foot. But being very docile and tame, they soon learn to return to call. When they have proved themselves sufficiently trustworthy, they are allowed to fish loose, with a leather strap round the neck, so that they cannot swallow the prey they have captured. When called, they return and disgorge it, and when they have thus secured as large a supply as their master wants, the strap is removed, and they are allowed to fish for themselves. The birds, when allowed a short rest at intervals, will continue their labours through the whole night, the fish being attracted to the boat, raft, or it may be plank fixed to the shore, by a torch kept burning.

Our hosts at Gifu were Mr. and Mrs. Chappell, of the Church Missionary Society, the station having been only taken up by the society about a year previously. Its origin is interesting. Mr. Chappell's brother was English teacher in the Government High School here, and being an earnest Christian man, devoted what time he could to drawing towards the Gospel those whom he could reach. The governor refused to allow him to hold services or to preach, but at length gave him permission, on condition of his promising not to speak against Buddha. This was a great step forward, considering that Mr. Chappell was a servant of the government. He then persuaded his brother, who was a curate in England, to come out and take his place, and he for some time supported the infant mission, and after an interval the Church Missionary Society adopted it. The result of two and a half years' work in a city where there was not a single baptized Christian to begin with, is that now there are seven out-stations, at three of which there are mission-rooms, in the others meetings in houses. There are two catechists continually at work, one at Gifu, the other in the villages. We met them both, and very earnest, capable men they appeared to be. In Gifu there were sixty-five Church members, besides eight baptized converts scattered in the out-stations. A good-sized hired house in a lovely garden served for a church, and as the garden gates stand open and the whole front of the church is also open, the people can stroll in here, and see as they like, without disturbing the services or committing themselves. The church was all matted, and much larger than that at Nagoya, but—which is quite an innovation for a strictly native community—had benches. There was a neat communion table, desks, and font. I had not yet met with a more promising infant church than this, but the people are characteristically independent, and Mr. Chappell knows what a parochial council means. A notice tablet by the gate gave a goodly list of the services and meetings throughout the week.

Gifu is dominated by a fine bold ridge of thickly-wooded hills, which we attempted to climb, but after a long scramble in the woods had to abandon the attempt, though we were rewarded by a grand view over the wide Ohari plain. We returned through a pretty public park, with band-stand and all the most modern appliances. After purchasing, as in duty bound, a due supply of paper and bamboo lanterns and fans, in most of which the cormorant fishing figures, we found a number of the Christians had assembled to meet us. I gave them an address, which was interpreted by one of the catechists, who understood English very fairly.

At Gifu we found ourselves off the Tōkaidō and on the Nakasendo, the other great road between Tokio and Kioto, leading mainly through the mountains, as its name implies, the Tōkaidō following the plain as far as possible. The road was constructed more than a thousand years ago. Tradition carries its origin much further back, and says that in the reign of the Emperor Kaiko, A.D. 71, his son made use of this road for the conquest of the eastern parts of Japan. I can hardly leave Gifu without mentioning that a very few months after our visit this fair country, with the lovely plain on which we had been gazing, and the vast city of Nagoya, were desolated, and Gifu itself destroyed by the earthquake, one of the most disastrous on record, and of the effects of which the illustrations may give some idea.

A long railway journey took us from Gifu to Hikone Station; but let not the weary traveller who is set down at the station imagine that he has arrived at the place, for in Japan, as elsewhere, stations are sometimes far from the spot whose name they bear. We found ourselves deposited at a roadside station late at night, with no means of conveyance for ourselves or our baggage to the town, until through the good offices of the kindly folk at the station kurumas were sent for, which landed us towards midnight at a little inn on the shores of Lake Biwa, where, having knocked up the people, we had tea, and slept soundly on the matted floor. Notwithstanding the shortness of our night, we pushed aside our paper screens soon after sunrise, and looked out on the fairy-like scene over the water. The house reminded us of the one at Hakone, pro-

KISOGAWA RIVER.

jecting over the lake, close to the little wooden pier, which already presented a busy scene, as bales of rice and fish were carried down ready for the steamer which runs the length of the lake twice a day, Hikone being a third of the way down on the western side. Biwa is larger than the Lake of Geneva, over thirty-six miles long, and surrounded by mountains on all sides, on one only of which did we notice the patches of snow remaining. There are several wooded islets scattered over it. The name is derived from a fancied resemblance to the shape of the guitar. The natives are very proud of this lake, which in their estimation ranks only second to Mount Fuji as one of the glories of Japan, and they are fond of boasting that it is larger than any lake in Europe. The tradition is that the lake was created by an earthquake in the year B.C. 286, at the same time that Fuji rose from the plains of Suruga. In Japanese poetry this lake is a favourite theme, and the 'eight beauties of Omi' (*i.e.* Biwa) are frequently alluded to, these beauties being the autumn moon as seen from one place, the evening sun from another, and so on. However fanciful these may be, no one who has seen it will deny that the lake presents many lovely landscapes, though none possess the grand or the sublime.

Hikone possesses a half-destroyed feudal castle, the seat of one of the Daimios, which would have been entirely demolished had not the Mikado, happening to pass through Hikone, and finding the inhabitants exhibiting, as they thought, their loyalty, by pulling down the noble old building, promptly stopped this act of vandalism. Unfortunately, at the time of the inauguration of the new era and the abolition of feudalism, loyalty was exhibited by the destruction of the old castles throughout the country, much as zeal for the Reformation was demonstrated by the destruction of abbeys.

As the steamer started from the north end of the lake, two or three hours before it reached Hikone, we had an opportunity for a stroll on the beach; and amongst the reeds and rushes I collected many splendid specimens of fresh-water shells, of species peculiar, I believe, to this district. Though generally the Japanese thoroughly appreciate a collector's taste, especially in botany, the villagers were exceedingly amused and perplexed by the interest we took in shells, and especially in those whose inmates were too small to eat, and which involved wading in the mud to find them.

At length the steamer arrived, more like a small steam launch than a passenger boat. All on board were Japanese, and there were a great many passengers. We had no idea of investigating the cabins, in which no person over five foot could enjoy locomotion excepting on all fours. But the captain, who at once made our acquaintance, could talk a little English, of which he was very proud, and was delighted to point out objects of interest during the few hours we were on board. He startled us by telling us that the Czarevitch had been nearly murdered by a policeman the day before at Otsu, at the south end of the lake, whither we were then on our way, and that he had been carried to Kioto. The man had struck him over the head and neck, and would certainly have killed him had not two kuruma men seized him. The consternation and excitement of the passengers may be imagined. The prominent feeling seemed to be distress at the disgrace that had thus been brought on their country, and that they would be looked upon as savages by other nations. To nothing is a Japanese so sensitive as to the suspicion that his nation is not looked upon as civilised, and therefore they felt keenly as a national slur the appearance of treachery to a guest.

Nearing Otsu, we passed close in shore by Karasaki, and could examine at our leisure the celebrated pine-tree, said to be the largest, not the tallest, of its kind in the world. Its branches spread downwards and outwards on all sides, many of them being close to the ground. The height of the tree is said to be 90 feet, the circumference of the trunk 37 feet, and the diameter covered by its branches from north to south 290, and from east to west 240 feet. The branches, of course, are all propped and supported, so that the tree has the appearance of a very flattened banyan. It is evidently carefully tended, and any signs of decay are promptly treated.

Arrived at the extremity of the lake, we found the town of Otsu in a ferment of excitement. It is a bustling, thriving little place, with wide streets, and a fine aqueduct, which has just been completed to convey the water thence to Kioto. It was to visit these works that the Czarevitch had come, when he was struck at by the policeman as he was returning from the formal opening of the tunnel. This tunnel, an example of bold engineering, pierces the mountain which bars the south end of Biwa. The tragic event took place exactly in front of the hotel where we rested, and the spot was being guarded by police. The would-be assassin was high in the force, over forty years of age, and had won distinction in the suppression of the Satsuma rebellion. He had been specially trusted with the care of the road for the passage of the Czarevitch. It is believed that he did the deed as a protest in revenge for the filching of Saghalien by Russia, a piece of Muscovite diplomacy which Japan has never forgiven. He probably belonged to a secret society, and was appointed by lot to commit the crime. He had on him a stiletto to kill himself, but was prevented by being instantly seized by two kuruma men. But the secret history of the affair will never be known, as no Japanese conspirator will ever, under any torture, betray another. The Czarevitch was at once taken to Kioto, and on learning the news by telegraph, the Mikado at once started from Tokio to visit him. The people of all ranks were horror-struck, and one old lady in Otsu on hearing it at once committed suicide by harakiri, to show her indignation.

As we dined sitting on the floor, while our landlord chatted very freely and retailed all the gossip on the event of the day, we could not help feeling how strange it was that here we were, the two solitary

Europeans in a country town in the interior of Japan, the name of which had scarcely ever been heard before out of the country, and yet that on this morning the name of Otsu would be in every newspaper and every mouth throughout the whole civilised world.

The only lion of Otsu besides the new aqueduct is a famous Buddhist temple sacred to Kwannon, the goddess of mercy, from which there is a lovely view of the lake, with the town in the foreground. It is not a very fatiguing walk to Kioto, and certainly no one who can walk should indulge in the questionable luxury of a kuruma for this expedition. Taking a coolie with us, we first examined the entrance of the aqueduct into the tunnel, two miles long, and then, passing by the temple, we had a charming walk over an easy pass. On our way were several air-shafts piercing the hill for the ventilation of the tunnel.

When, having descended the hill, we emerged on the high road, we could well imagine the scene on the Tōkaidō before the introduction of railways. Dusty indeed and crowded it was, but it gave us an opportunity of noticing the great variety of type amongst the country people; not less was the variety of the ingenious modes of carrying every kind of market and garden produce into this vast city. The peasantry do not show their gallantry in the matter of female labour, for a great part of the firewood was being brought into the town in huge bundles on the heads of the women, and women were tugging at the carts alongside of oxen.

We lost the first impression of Kioto, as the sun had set, and had a weary tramp of two miles through the streets before we reached our intended hotel, reputed to be one of the best native hotels in Japan. To our dismay, we found that it was impossible to secure the humblest shelter here, for, as the landlord assured us, the crowd of the Mikado's suite had covered every mat. The landlord was an old acquaintance of my daughter, and, most anxious to serve us, recommended us to another hotel—alike in vain. We trudged on, to be shut out, homeless wanderers, everywhere. Dead tired, we at last betook ourselves to kurumas, and finally, at ten o'clock, in a remote part of the city found an inn, where they said they could give us one small room between us, and promised a paper screen to divide it, for they too were crammed with visitors. There was no help for it, unless we were prepared to spend the night in the streets.

COLOSSAL IMAGE OF BUDDHA.

CHAPTER VI

A SECOND VISIT TO KIOTO

To know and understand Kioto would require a residence of many weeks; to describe it adequately, a volume of many pages. Short as was my time in Japan, the few days that in the first instance I gave to Kioto were so utterly insufficient that I was glad to have the opportunity of paying it a second visit on the eve of my departure, to supply some few of my many omissions. It is looked upon in Japan as the centre of the national life. For many centuries it was the gilded prison of the Mikado. It is emphatically a city of temples, and is still practically the religious metropolis of the nation. It fully justifies the reverence and admiration with which it is regarded by the people.

It lies in a plain at the foot of the great central range of mountains, which may be compared to our own Pennine range, in the narrowest part of Hondo, the main island of Japan. Easy mountain roads converge to it from all quarters. It is only forty miles from Osaka, formerly the great harbour of the eastern coast, with which it has water communication. The plain is surrounded on three sides by mountains clad in perpetual green. Branches of the river Yodogawa meander through the city, shaded with ancient trees; and though the streets are formal in their arrangement, running parallel and at right angles, yet the monotony is broken by the continually recurring gardens, groves and temples. Pagodas and shrines dot the mountain side, and the lower slopes are brightened by the variegated hues of innumerable gardens. But withal Kioto seems to tell one that its glories are of the past. It is the one city of Japan which shows at once that it has shrunken within its ancient limits, and ancient streets and squares are now transformed into suburban parks and fields. This has been the natural and necessary result of the transference of power from the Shogun to the Mikado, and the change of residence of the latter to Tokio, which is more and more the centre of national life.

Kioto is, however, so continually visited by travellers and described by writers that my impressions are not likely to convey anything novel. We had the good fortune to see it *en fête*, inasmuch as the emperor with his whole court arrived a few hours after ourselves to show his sympathy with the Czarevitch, and although we had secured our quarters, there was no sleep in Kioto that night. The emperor was expected about midnight, the whole city was illuminated, the national flag, white with the red rising sun in the centre, hung over every door, and a large paper lantern bearing the same colours was suspended beneath it. All the public buildings were lighted up with the electric light, and the result of the red and white winkling stars beneath the electric blaze was very effective. The perpetual din, coming and going, ceaseless talking all night, banished sleep, and once I was roused by a visit from a policeman in search of a culprit.

When we rose in the morning, our first question was naturally for the bath-room, inasmuch as there is no basin or convenience for washing in a Japanese room. All ablutions and toilet are performed outside. The reply was, 'No bath here, for the bath-room is filled with boxes, but there is a very good bath opposite.' But 'opposite' we soon found meant half-way down the street on the other side. There was nothing for it but to set off in slippers and dressing gown, towel and sponge in hand, to find it. Arrived, we found three or four baths in front of a kitchen, all open to the public, and each already occupied by at least one bather. The attendants offered, however, to run a slide to screen them from the street, but they could not provide a separate bath for each. Baulked and unwashed, we returned, and after some negotiation got tubs placed in a back garden. Having now returned to the abode of rank and fashion, we were obliged to look after the affairs of our wardrobe. A Chinaman who had a board opposite the hotel, announcing in pidgin English, 'Washman from Kobe,' introduced himself, followed by his rival, who asserted that he was 'wase man.' At length, attired in travelling best, we went to deliver introductions and cards, and to inquire at the hotel where the Czarevitch was staying. We found that his imperial highness had already gone down to Kobe, accompanied by the emperor, who escorted him on board a Russian man-of-war. Thus prematurely was the imperial visit cut short.

Distances are so great in Kioto that we were glad to engage kurumas by the day. Our first visit was to the Buddhist temples of Hongwanji, belonging to the purest sect, for we must remember that there are as many sects among them as in Christendom. This sect of the Shinshu has been already mentioned as being characterised by teaching the doctrine of justification by faith, not works. One of the leading priests here is an Oxford graduate, a member of Balliol College, who has recently written a work advancing further than this sect in general, and repudiating works of merit, since no man can justify himself or wash out his own past sins, but must rely on Buddha's righteousness, and do good works as fruits and proofs of faith. In the western Hongwanji temple there are many empty shrines with figures of great saints depicted on the walls, but no images excepting a very small wooden image, about two feet high, of the founder of the sect in the chancel, and in the dependent temple adjoining a gilt wooden figure of the Amida incarnation of Buddha about three feet high.

The temple and its annexes, for they are really a series of great halls, give one rather the idea of picture galleries than of places of worship. I should have mentioned before a fine sacred tree in the courtyard in front, the *Gingko biloba*, which is believed to protect the temple against

TEMPLE AT KIOTO (SEE P. 207).

fire by discharging showers of water whenever there is a conflagration in the neighbourhood. On the walls hang many a kakemono, *i.e.* hanging painted scrolls, glorifying Buddha, and also portraits of great divines, some of them said to be more than two or three centuries old. Most attractive in one of the great halls was a series of beautiful pictures of snow scenes on the sliding panels. One set represented the snow on pines, another on plum-trees, another on bamboos. The execution is admirable, whatever may be said of the perspective. A very favourite flower in the decoration and carvings of this temple is the tree peony, which competes for distinction in these designs with the imperial chrysanthemum. One hall was surrounded with representations of flocks of geese in every conceivable position on a gold ground. All these paintings, perfectly preserved as they are, seem to have been painted, not on the panels, but on paper which has been afterwards glued to the panels. One could not but regret that the effect of this magnificent group of buildings, whose architecture is so characteristic, is somewhat marred by a large adjacent structure, which has recently been erected in what is imagined to be European style. These buildings are a college for young priests, and also a girls' school, the intention being to supply a liberal education on modern lines, combined with training in the reformed Buddhism.

Close by this temple is another cathedral edifice, the eastern Hongwanji, which is as yet unfinished, although it has been thirty years in rebuilding after the destruction of the ancient temple by fire. When completed it will be the largest temple in Japan, and it differs from almost every other temple in having its walls of massive masonry. Before it is finished, it is computed that it will have cost about a million

A JAPANESE LADY.

dollars. Whatever may be thought of the decay of Buddhism in general, there is certainly life and zeal in the Hongwanji sect, if we may judge by the voluntary offerings given not only by the rich, but by the poor, and that through the length and breadth of the nation. Many of the poorest have given both their personal labour and gifts of material. Amongst the most remarkable evidences of devotion are the contributions of something like 250,000 women, who gave their hair as an offering to Buddha, to make the ropes employed in hoisting the great stones of the outer walls into their places. We saw fifty-three of these ropes of rich glossy black hair, each two spans in circumference. I am unable to state the length of each, but should think it was probably forty or fifty feet. When we know how the women of the country prize their hair, and the pains they take in arranging their rich black tresses, we cannot but recognise the devoted zeal which has impelled them to such a sacrifice. I should add that this temple has been built without any subvention from the state. The carvings of the ceiling and of the cornices, which were in course of execution, certainly show no falling off in the boldness and accuracy of Japanese art.

But I will not weary my readers by the monotonous iteration of descriptions of Japanese temples, which are so uniform in general character. Our second day's sojourn we devoted to lionising the east side of Kioto. Here the city extends close to the foot of a mountain range, which is densely wooded to the bottom. It forms, in fact, a background rising immediately from the termination of the streets. Buried among the trees, high up and low down, are countless temples. Crowds of pilgrims, with their palmer's dress and great umbrella hat; beggar children whining after us, 'The eating thing I cannot do,' meaning that they have nothing to eat, and are ready for donations, fill every path. Walking up by the side of a cyclopean wall, we turned to see the celebrated Daibutsu (great Buddha), whose sacred enclosure is surrounded by this magnificent masonry. The Daibutsu owes its origin to the hero Hideyoshi, a little more than three hundred years ago. It has unfortunately more than once been destroyed by fire and earthquake, the two enemies of historic monuments in Japan. The original image was of bronze, destroyed by an earthquake. The present, a wooden one, which is only a hundred years old, consists simply of the head and shoulders of the sage. Some idea of its colossal size may be gained by a statement of the measurements, the height of the image being 60 feet, the face 30 feet long, the eyebrows 8 feet, and the shoulders 43 feet across. Gigantic as it is, if one can examine it from a sufficient distance, it will be seen that the conventional placidity of expression is most perfectly rendered. Outside is hung the great bell, weighing over 60 tons, and one of the largest in Japan.

In another temple, the Sanju-Sangendō, containing 33,333 images of Kwannon, the goddess of mercy, are long corridors. There are 1,001 images of the goddess, life-size, and all gilded, placed tier behind tier. They are all the work of artists celebrated in history, and it is boasted that in not one of the thousand and one are the face or position of the hands or arrangement of the articles that they hold identical. The differences, however, are often very slight. The number 33,333 is made up by

RICE IMAGES, JAPAN.

reckoning all the smaller figures which are in the ornamentation, especially those on the gilded haloes which surround each head. In the centre of the temple is a large seated figure of Kwannon, surrounded by eight-and-twenty of her traditional followers. In the days of archery, the great triumph of a Japanese bowman was to be able to send an arrow from one end to the other of the verandah of this building. The cost of the statues of this temple must be fabulous.

Near this is a Shinto temple, without any images, but with the shrine simply occupied by a large mirror, encircled by two wreaths of white paper. To see the immense variety of temples on this mountain side, devoted to all kinds of hideous idols, to incarnations of Buddha, to gods of thunder, rain, wealth, pleasure, to the gods of every kind of disease, gives some idea of the strange divergence of practical Buddhism from the ideal theories which are propounded as Buddhism in the West. The children's Buddhist temple is worthy of a visit. It contains any number of small wooden Buddhas, arranged in shelves sloping back, tier over tier, and covered with the baby clothes of infants who have died under a year old. One of the most remarkable and beautiful of these temples, that of Kiyomigu, is a vast structure erected on a great framework, leaning, as it were, against the steep side of the mountain. The framework, as will be seen from the illustration on page 199, is many storeys high, and the roof is thatched. It is on one side of the ravine, with a similar but smaller temple facing it on the other side. Looking down from the platform, this dell gives the impression of a veritable abyss. Wide corridors encircle the temple on all four sides. The outer court is merely separated from them by the supporting columns of the roof, so that it is practically one vast open hall. At the further end is a long matted corridor, and within that the holy of holies, which contains the shrines, and where lights are kept burning. We had just left this temple when an unexpected rainfall drove us into a pagoda, which we could ascend, and under the verandah of the upper storey we opened our lunch bag and rested, with the magnificent panorama of the city and its plain in front. I could not regret that our temple-trotting was arrested by the rain, for two days of countless Buddhas and thousands of Kwannons had pretty well exhausted me, and even the finest works of art when too often repeated become monotonous.

As a contrast to the temple-covered mountain, next day we rode to the Dōshisha, the earliest and greatest missionary educational institution in Japan, and of which the famous Joseph Neeshima, one of the earliest and most eminent of Japanese Christians, was principal until his death, the year before our visit. It was founded in 1875 by the American Board of Missions. I little expected to find so vast a collection of buildings. The grounds and halls cover many acres. There is a fine lofty chapel, a library of three thousand English volumes, halls and schools for theoretical and practical chemistry, physical science lecture halls with splendid apparatus, dining halls,

a theological department; all separate buildings in Western, not Japanese style, none of them excepting the chapel having any architectural pretensions. There are also dormitories for four hundred students, professors' houses and gardens; in fact, a complete university in itself. The chemistry hall was built and furnished in 1890 by the gift of $100,000 from an American visitor, and another $100,000 was recently left it for the encouragement of physical studies by a Boston Unitarian. The larger part of the students are non-Christian, but under Christian influences and teaching many are continually seeking baptism. The theological schools are very well organised. Dr. Gordon, the senior professor, took us over every department, and asked the native principal, Mr. Neeshima's successor, to meet us at dinner. This is a grand piece of missionary work on a large scale, and quite equal in its educational equipment to the Jesuit College of Tou-sè-wè, near Shanghai.

We also visited the training college for nurses, which is under the management of the same mission. The hospital is small, but is large enough for its purpose, which is simply the training of nurses, and all the probationers as well as the nurses are Christians.

One can hardly speak of the Dōshisha without referring to the story of Joseph Neeshima's life. Long before the opening of Japan to either commerce or Christianity, Neeshima somehow got hold of a Chinese geography book compiled for a mission school, and beginning with the words, 'In the beginning God created the heavens and the earth.' To the Buddhist student, who had never known any other faith, this was a startling discovery. What could it mean? Who was that God? Certainly He did not live in Japan. Perhaps He might live in America, whence the author of the book came. So at the peril of his life, for it was at that time death for a Japanese to leave his country, he made his way in a trader to China, and thence obtained a passage to Boston. Then he explained his errand to the captain who had brought him. 'I came all this way,' said he, 'to find God, and there is no one to tell me.' The captain took him to the owner, a wealthy Christian merchant, who received him as a son, and sent him to college. Eleven years afterwards, in 1875, he returned to Japan as a missionary under the American Board, and became president of the Dōshisha College, just then founded.

This Dōshisha was the earliest college for higher education in Kioto, but after some years was followed by one of the three upper grade colleges maintained by the government, originally established in Osaka, but later removed to Kioto. Its buildings are in another suburb of the city, and though useful, are certainly not ornamental. It has often perplexed me why the Japanese, whose taste both in art and dress is perfect in their own style, when they attempt foreign style, whether it be in dress or architecture, not only do not approach the beautiful, but generally achieve the absolutely ugly. We had here the advantage of being the guests of Professor Sharpe, who is pronounced by the Japanese to be the best English professor in Japan, and whose warm hospitality, rich fund of information and cultured criticism made our visit one of the most charming reminiscences of the tour.

The passion for industrial exhibitions has reached Japan, or probably, a patriot would tell us, originated there. The Imperial Exhibition at Kioto, just now open, was a very European looking affair, and practically nothing but a great bazaar. Its great attraction was that the purchaser of a ticket for admission could through it obtain admission to what are called the Gardens of the Empress, and for visiting which this ticket was indispensable. The Mikado by this concession very substantially patronised the exhibition, and ensured its success. My visit to it gave me an opportunity of purchasing at very little cost small sets of tools of the various trades, carpenters, bookbinders, engravers, etc., which by their striking originality and contrast with our own are most valuable illustrations of Japanese art. As Kioto is a great centre for porcelain manufacture, we had opportunities of watching parts of the process of production, and of laying in a store of choice vases for wedding presents. The part of the building best worth a visit was the department illustrative of the silk and embroidery manufacture, in which also Kioto is pre-eminent. Scarfs, silk handkerchiefs and embroideries for screens of great delicacy and richness, in which I suppose Japan is unrivalled, must extract from any visitor of taste his last available yen.

The Empress' Gardens, so named because they are attached to what was formerly the palace of the empress, are still at ordinary times looked on as the emperor's private grounds, and not at all as a public park. There is no great variety of flowers or shrubs, but the labyrinths, artificial liliputian mountains, ornamental waters, and lovely shaded walks with noble trees most artistically arranged, are its special features. Four wonderful specimens of wistaria, now one blaze of blossom, shaded the whole length of a very long bridge across an artificial lake. The wistaria at home I should be almost inclined to place before the cherry as the brightest floral glory of Japan. One seldom sees it in such masses as in this garden; but it is abundant in all the forests, where its effect as it shoots its climbing branches from tree to tree, laden and apparently weighed down with rich purple clusters of bloom, contrasts magnificently with the azaleas, red, white and pink, below it. Nor is its effect less when, in the absence of forest tree to support it, it contents itself with forming a massive shrub not unlike a luxuriant blackberry in its mode of growth.

We gave one day to rather a long expedition to the mountain known as Hieizan. The slopes of this mountain supply the favourite summer camping-ground of residents of Kioto and Osaka. Knowing it would be a long day's work, we took kurumas to the mountain foot. It was indeed a hot climb up the rugged path. We reached a summit, and at first fancied we had won our goal; but no, it was not the

WEAVING SILK.

summit. That was three miles further on. Fatiguing as the further climb was, the view of valleys on either side, and Kioto below us, its temples and gardens sprawling over a vast extent of plain, and wooded hills fringing the landscape beyond, with a peep of Lake Biwa, well repaid us. There was a little rest-shed on the way, but so full of rough men and boys that we were glad to find a pine-tree, which afforded some shade on the side of what was almost a precipice, where we contrived to sit and rest and enjoy the prospect as we lunched. I think the entomology on this mountain was the most varied I met with in the country.

Mount Hieizan also was the scene of many of the exploits of Benkei, the Japanese Samson. According to the legend, he was eight feet high, and as strong as a hundred men. One of his feats was to carry a great temple bell up the mountain, but on reaching the summit the bell continuously cried out, 'I want to go back, I want to go back,' whereupon he let it go rolling down to the mountain foot, where it may now be seen suspended in a temple In proof of the truth of the story, they show us the ravine which was ploughed out by the bell in its course from the top to the bottom of the mountain. On the mountain, amongst others, are two temples connected with each other by an arched gallery. The legend of these is that this was the yoke which Benkei wore on his shoulders, and by which he carried the twin temples and set them down where they now stand.

During the Middle Ages Hieizan was the sacred

mountain of Japanese Buddhism, and tradition raises the number of the temples which covered it to three thousand, containing many thousand warrior priests, who were nothing less than organised banditti, and were in the habit of making plundering excursions into the neighbouring country, taking part in the petty tribal wars of the different Daimios. It was not till about three hundred and fifty years ago that these monks, the terror of Kioto, were driven out of their strongholds, and all their temples and buildings burnt by the Shoguns. A century later the Tokugawa Shoguns allowed the monasteries to be re-established, but strictly limited their number. The mountain still has a special sanctity, and until recently there was a notice at its foot, 'No woman or cow permitted to ascend this mountain.' Near the summit are the impression of two colossal feet carved in the rock, held by the devout to be the impression of Buddha's feet when he descended to visit Japan. Its sanctity, however, did not prevent my securing a very fair take of butterflies, which were flitting about as innocent as myself of the veneration expected of pilgrims to these sacred heights, and were most interesting, as many of them represent our familiar English forms of *Vanessas*, tortoise-shells, and fritillaries; though, contrary to what happens in the case of mammals, the Japanese species seems to be always larger and finer than their European congeners.

As the Mikado and his suite were at Kioto at the period of our first visit, we were not able to see the private apartments of the palace, but felt it was fully worth while when at Osaka some weeks later to run over on purpose to inspect them, and well were we rewarded. A tall monotonous wall, covered with stucco and roofed with thatch, surrounds the park in which the cluster of buildings forming the palace stand. There are several gates, the centre one being never opened but for the Mikado himself. Passing the sentries and presenting our letter, we were admitted to a lodge within the gate, where we were met by a most courteous gentleman and old official of the Mikado, evidently a man of liberal education—a sort of hereditary chamberlain, as we presumed from his telling us that he succeeded his father in attendance on the late Mikado, and with natural pride he pointed out to us, as we passed through the palace, his own portrait in a large wall painting representing a grand annual procession. After signing our names in a large register, he conducted us across the grounds, which are beautifully kept in native fashion, to the reception-hall, only used on state occasions and festivals. The panels are covered with paintings, but the best pictures have been removed to Tokio, as the emperor does not often reside here. Here we were shown the Mikado's throne, with canopy and rich curtains of white, red, and black silk, within which the emperor used to be seated on a mat. The imperial badge of the chrysanthemum with sixteen petals was worked in everywhere, in cornices and curtains, and seemed to be repeated wherever there was space to receive it. Yet with all this, there was a strange air of desolation about these cold and silent chambers. In a second and much larger hall was a more modern throne, in which the emperor sat in a chair, enclosed in curtains of the richest silk, which only permitted his feet to be seen.

In front of this throne is a flight of eighteen wide steps leading to the great court below. Each of the steps corresponded to a particular rank of the old nobility. Officials not noble were obliged to stand on the earth below the lowest step, and great were the heartburnings amongst the Daimios, and many the feuds engendered, by one obtaining a higher grade than another on this staircase of rank. A long corridor led from this hall to the library or study of the palace, a very fine room with priceless lacquer boxes arranged on shelves to hold the emperor's books.

Our charming guide told us that he spent many hours a day with the late emperor here in his study, for he was a great student and very fond of geography. Though never able to go beyond the grounds of the palace, he was most curious as to what went on in the outside world, and used to ask all sorts of questions from his courtiers and attendants. Practically, with the exception of one or two annual processions, in which he was concealed, he never could go beyond the thirty acres of ground that composed the park and gardens of his palace. What an idea of gilded misery that palace gives one! The private chambers of the old Mikados, separated from the great hall, and the sliding screens of which were richly decorated, consist of eleven rooms, in which for six hundred years the successive Mikados have lived and died. The ordinary sitting-room was surrounded by the apartments of his female attendants, through whom alone a message could be taken to him, when he passed to a room at the other end, where he received his officials. Behind this are nine handsome bedrooms, with richly painted panels, the centre one being the emperor's, so that he is carefully secluded at night, as in the day. Our courtier guide told my daughter anecdotes of the late Mikado, and expressed his satisfaction at having for once to conduct a visitor who could converse in Japanese, as he generally had to go through his explanations in pantomime, for no guides or servants are permitted to cross the gates.

Our courteous friend told us that we ought to see the Castle of Nijo, or old Shogun's palace, to see which he would give us a letter to the chamberlain there. We parted with much ceremony, and when we told our men to take us to the castle they demurred, telling us it was of no use. We evidently rose in their estimation when on presenting our letter the sentry let us pass. A stately official received the document with a profound reverence, and preceded us within the precincts. Certainly the best had been kept to the last. It is by far the most palatial palace we had seen, surpassing Nagoya, with lavish decorations and gilding everywhere, but all in the best taste. It is larger than the palace, except for the great audience hall, and certainly the Shogun took care of himself at his superior's expense. Instead of the eighteen steps for the various ranks in the Mikado's palace, there were seven steps, on which according to their rank the highest Daimios could stand. The minor Daimios could not stand even on the lowest of these. It was very interesting to hear the account of all these old-world ceremonials from those who had themselves taken part in them. All the walls and ceilings were painted in panels, the series of subjects differing for each room and wonderfully ingenious. We may remark that its decorations are on a much larger and vaster scale than those I have seen elsewhere in the country. Each hall is named from the subject of its decoration. In the tiger hall there are perhaps a dozen tigers in different attitudes, and both the animals and the plants of the jungle are all represented life-size, as are the eagles and peacocks in other rooms. Everywhere was to be seen the gilt trefoil crest of the Tokugawa Shoguns, except in the one suite reserved for the Mikado, when once a year he came to visit him, and there the gold chrysanthemum is on every hinge and handle and panel. We were delighted with this grand old feudal castle. It is not a little amusing to observe the different opinions that are given concerning it. One guide book describes it as 'an old and dingy building'; another, as I venture to think much more truly, says, 'This palace, a dream of golden beauty within, is externally a good example of the Japanese fortress, with its turrets at the corners and its walls of cyclopean masonry. It is, however, only a fraction of its former self.'

CHAPTER VII

OSAKA

FROM Kioto to Osaka, from Edinburgh to Glasgow, from history, arts, and literature to commerce and manufactures! The train winds amongst hills for a few miles, then for the rest of the way down the valley of the Yodogawa, through paddy fields as uninteresting as Chatmoss. From the top of a hill midway between Kioto and Osaka both cities are plainly visible. À *propos* of this view, I may give an illustration of the Japanese Æsop. Once upon a time an Osaka frog, having heard the fame of the beauties of Kioto, thought he could not do better than migrate thither. Another frog resident in Kioto heard wonderful tales of the bustle and liveliness of Osaka, and wearied of Kioto, determined to change his home. Meeting at the top of the hill, where each hoped to obtain a view of the paradise to which he was bound, they raised themselves up full of eager expectation, forgetting that in that posture a frog looks backward. 'Well, really,' said the dweller among the Osaka swamps, 'Kioto looks uncommonly like Osaka, and every bit as flat. I could not do better than go home again.' 'So that is Osaka,' exclaimed the resident of the capital; 'how wonderfully similar it is to Kioto! I don't see that I should be the gainer by proceeding.' And both frogs returned home well satisfied, and with no desire to pursue their acquaintance with the outer world. Moral—Don't look at everything through your own spectacles.

Osaka, with a population of nearly half a million, is the second city in the empire, and whilst being the Manchester of Japan, is at the same time an ancient city, and first came into prominence in the sixteenth century, when Hideyoshi, who has been called the Napoleon of Japan, made it his fortress and capital. But he has greater claims on the respect and admiration of Europe than even his development of the commerce of Osaka and his extension of the Japanese empire, for amongst many wise measures of internal policy he gave toleration to the Christians, and it was under his rule that the Roman Catholic missions were spread over the whole country. His favourite general and many of his best troops were Christians, and with them he invaded and endeavoured to conquer Corea, as a step to the subjugation of China. He succeeded in utterly crushing the independence and also, alas! the civilisation of Corea, but failed to make any impression upon the Flowery Land. Since his invasion of Corea, although after his death the Japanese troops were withdrawn, the peninsula seems to have sunk into still lower depths of degradation; and the nation which was once the instructress of Japan in art, and the masterpieces of some of whose artists still exist, has sunk to such a state as to have earned from a recent well known traveller the character of being the dregs of humanity.

The Castle of Osaka, which still exists, was commenced by Hideyoshi in 1583, and was completed in two years. It was said to be the strongest fortress in the country, as the palace which it contained was the most magnificent. The encircling wall and the sides of the moat are composed of masonry twenty feet thick, in the cyclopean style, without mortar and with no filling in, but solid throughout. The finest specimens of these huge stones are near the principal gateway. There is an amusing tradition of the stratagem by which Hideyoshi obtained his materials cheaply. He proclaimed over the whole country his intention of building this fortress, and announced an enormous prize to be given to the man who should produce the largest stone. The prize was great enough to tempt all classes, from the greatest Daimios downwards, and the largest junks that could be obtained were despatched from every part of the empire freighted with massive fragments of rock to the harbour of Osaka. In due time the prize was awarded, but to only one amongst many hundred competitors. The unsuccessful rivals were told they might carry their stones back again, but this permission, not being remunerative, was not taken advantage of, and Hideyoshi obtained materials and carriage free of cost. The castle was captured thirty years after its erection by Iyeyasu, and its memory must be ever preserved as that of the place where in 1868

Iyeyasu's descendant, the last of the Tokugawa Shoguns, received the members of the foreign legations and for the last time exercised the usurped imperial power.

Compelled to abandon it the same year, the Shogun's retainers before departing set it on fire, and in a few hours the grandest building in Japan was a heap of smouldering ruins. The fortifications now serve as the headquarters of the military district, and an artillery depôt and barracks have been erected on the site of the ancient keep or donjon, the one remaining feature of which is a deep and copious well capable of supplying the whole garrison in time of siege.

From the summit we had an unbroken view of the whole of this Oriental Venice, with its six hundred bridges and canals, a complete network, and the plain beyond, bounded by two ranges of hills. The number of tall factory chimneys standing out in the distance were a striking contrast to the gardens which varied a similar panorama of Kioto, and were certainly not congruous with the associations of the historic ramparts within which we were standing. One fact of interest in connection with the Castle of Osaka is that here for the last time the national practice of harakiri, or suicide, was permitted as a favour to criminals of honourable birth in lieu of decapitation. Twelve Samurai, who were sentenced to death for the murder of a French sailor, claimed this privilege in 1868.

With the castle we have done with the historic

features of Osaka; for its popular sights—the mint, the match factories, the cotton mills, the iron foundries, the timber yards—attractive though they may be to the merchant, are not what we have crossed three oceans to see.

But one temple should be mentioned, Tennōji, a large group of buildings in fine, park-like grounds, one of which is the children's temple. At its shrine were hundreds of children's clothes, hanging from ceiling to floor on pegs and on little figures of Buddha, and babies' bibs covered the bell-ropes. These were all the garments of deceased infants offered by the mothers. A priest sitting on a mat gives the bereaved mother, for a fee, a shaving of wood with the name of the dead child written on it. This she takes to another shrine, where is a pool of water issuing from the mouth of a colossal stone tortoise. The pool is full of these slips. They are cast into it just where the water pours in from the tortoise's mouth, and happy is the woman whose slip gets well soaked at once. It is believed that this will ensure the child an easy passage to heaven, as the water conveys the name to Buddha, who at once calls for them as he reads them.

To me, naturally, the attractions of Osaka centred in the vast and successful missionary work which is there carried on. In the narrow district of which Osaka is the centre, and the population of which is over a million, there are six American missionary organizations at work and one English, the Church Missionary Society, which has a very complete and extensive organization. All these are working in perfect harmony without the least friction, as well they may in a city of half a million, besides the suburbs. Besides these is a French Roman Catholic mission. It may give some idea of missionary life here to describe my experiences of Whit Sunday at Osaka. I was lodged in the Bishop Poole Memorial School, a large boarding-school for giving higher education on a Christian basis to Japanese girls of the middle and upper classes, over which my daughter presides, founded in memory of Bishop Poole, the first Anglican missionary bishop. After breakfasting at half-past seven o'clock, we made our way into a very poor part of the city, where my daughter holds a Sunday school. We were accompanied by one of the native teachers and three of the elder girls, who here take classes, and are thus beginning to train for missionary work. The school was a poor woman's dwelling-house. Partitions had all been cleared away, and furniture there was none, and thus the three rooms of which the house consisted were thrown into one. As soon as the singing and prayer were over, the teachers squatted on the mats, each with her class in a semicircle. Some of the mothers accompanied their children. It happened that on this very morning the first-fruits of this little mission were reaped, when a woman stayed behind and applied to be prepared for baptism, and also to bring to the font her two little children. She accompanied us to the native service, that she might be introduced to Mr. Terasawa, the native clergyman,

JAPANESE GIRLS, WRITING, SEWING, AND READING.

as a catechumen. Mr. Terasawa is the pastor of Trinity (not Trinity Chapel), our oldest native church, a large, well-built structure, quite in the native style, yet unmistakably ecclesiastical. An English missionary read prayers in Japanese, and Mr. Terasawa preached. There were two adult baptisms, one the wife of a judge, a leading man of rank here, who himself is also looking for baptism; the other, a clerk in a government office. One of my daughter's pupils was to be baptized, but as an infant, at the evening service. There were about seventy communicants—more than half the adult congregation. Service over, we went by invitation to morning tea at the parsonage next door. Mr. Terasawa's wife speaks English well, and her husband, though not able to converse fluently, is able to read English well, and had a well-selected, if small, English theological library in his quaint little study. I did not visit the afternoon school, as I had an opportunity of joining in English worship at Trinity College, in a very neat college chapel, which would not have discredited an English university, and was built from the designs of one of our missionaries, Mr. Pole. The congregation numbered about fifty, and all, excepting the English head of the Japanese Concession Police, belonged to the families either of our own or the American missionaries.

In the evening I went with Mr. Fyson, one of our pioneer missionaries, who was to take the preaching at a mission-room. This was one kept up by Miss Holland, a lady who, unconnected with any society, devotes herself, at her own cost, to helping mission work. She had argued that in a country where the people are not familiar with the Sabbath day's rest, there were many who would like to hear something of Christianity, but might be told, 'This is not the preaching night,' and so might delay or forget. But if there was preaching every night, no chance would be missed. She therefore hired a house close to some markets in a very busy street, put in a harmonium, got the place new matted, hung bright pictures of the Religious Tract Society all round the walls, got a large lantern, projecting in front, with the announcement on the transparent paper on one side, 'Teaching of Christ to-night,' and on the other were depicted a cross and a crown. She engaged an old woman to look after the place, and open and light it every evening. She gets one or two friends to help her with the singing, and has managed to secure a preacher, native or foreign, lay or cleric, every evening for months. For some time, when the venture was first started, the noise and jeering sometimes almost stopped the preacher. But that phase, inevitable at the beginning of every such work, had nearly passed over. When we arrived we found the three matted rooms packed full, and a crowd standing ten deep in the street. After a hymn, started by two English ladies, Mr. Fyson, standing at the edge of the room, held the people for over half an hour by what seemed to me a torrent of eloquence as he spoke of Pentecost. Texts on the subject, painted in great letters on kakemonos, were hung in front, so that all could read. After singing again, I too was expected to speak, and a more difficult task than addressing a crowd with an interpreter I never had, and I think it is impossible to be interesting under such conditions. There may have been two hundred listeners, and the meetings here have already been the means of bringing not a few into the Christian fold. There are many such preaching-places in Osaka, but what are they amongst half a million?

Nor are these efforts confined to the city itself. I walked out with my daughter one afternoon to a similar meeting three miles from the outskirts of the city, to a so-called village of three thousand souls, employed in making coarse pottery and farming. We had a most uninteresting walk first through narrow streets and past factory chimneys, and then along a raised path through paddy fields till we reached a broad river, and were ferried across to the village. As I turned round I counted from one spot sixty-two factory chimneys, for this is becoming the great cotton-spinning centre. The use of a house was hired for this weekly meeting, to which the head teacher and three senior pupils went with us, to carry the picture and help in the singing. The rooms of the house being thrown together, about sixty people, chiefly women, soon assembled. Slipping off our shoes at the door, we passed to the inner end, which was open to the garden. A large coloured print of the Ascension was unrolled and pinned up, and a hymn was sung, only joined in by the visitors.

Then the teacher spoke for half an hour, then again there was singing, which always attracts these people, another address from my daughter explaining the Ascension, and then singing and prayer concluded the meeting. This is a new mission, and there are no Christians yet, but several are interested, and the people were all very quiet and attentive. This is the simple way in which out-stations begin, and the seed is sown. On our return we halted at a tea-house in a village where there was formerly a similar meeting, until the Buddhist priest interfered and threatened any one who should lend their house for the purpose. This is the kind of local opposition which we must always expect from time to time; but what is this compared to the resistance of the Irish priesthood?

There being no division of days into weeks in this country is at first a difficulty, but for convenience' sake, since the increase of foreign trade, the government have made Sunday a *dies non* in all schools, government offices, and other official places. But the people generally have hardly got familiarised with this, and adhere to their old division into ten days, holding a night fair in various parts of the town every fifth day. Advantage is taken of these evenings for special preaching.

What is called the Concession is a district assigned to the foreigners in each treaty port when the country was first opened, and where alone they are allowed to hold land. But as the river at Osaka is much silted up, and is of no use for ocean-going vessels, the large shipping has entirely deserted it and dropped down to Kobe, twenty miles off, which is practically the seaport of Osaka. The merchants, with hardly an exception, have abandoned the large and spacious houses which they had built, till the whole foreign population of Osaka is limited to the various missionary bodies, who have had the opportunity of securing quarters which they would not have built for themselves. The principal English Mission institutions, besides the girls' school already mentioned, are Trinity College, for the training of theological students; a large boys' boarding school, in a distant part of the city, intended to provide for the boys the same style of education which the Bishop Poole School affords to their sisters; and the Bible Women's training home, a most important part of the work, where not only the women are trained to be missionaries to their sisters throughout the country, but during their training are useful in the work in Osaka.

The boys' high school, which is four miles from the Concession, had not at the time of our visit been long in operation; yet, though it has to compete with the government school, it had at the time of our visit, besides day scholars, thirty-eight boarders, but is calculated for the accommodation of a hundred and twenty, and by special subscriptions raised for the purpose admirable apparatus has been supplied, and the dining-hall, class-rooms, bath-rooms and dormitories are all in keeping, and the school is under the able direction of Mr. Price, son of a veteran African missionary.

But, perhaps, looking to the future, the most important of our institutions is Trinity College. There are usually between twenty and thirty students. The third year of their four-years' course is spent in practical catechist's work in the country, a most important part of their training. It is a very complete Divinity College. Its excellent buildings leave nothing to be desired. The street façade is of brick, plain but handsome, and on either side of the doorway is a Japanese inscription cut in the stone, and which may be literally translated, 'The one-God-in-three teaching-house.' Within is a quadrangle which has quite an Oxford air, one side formed by the chapel, another by the principal's house, and the other two by the dining-hall and lecture-rooms downstairs, the dormitories with deep verandahs being upstairs. There are four lecture-rooms, a small library of standard theology, and the vice-principal's sitting-room. Behind the quadrangle are the bath-rooms, kitchens and offices with abundant space.

Our last Sunday in Osaka was a red-letter day, being that of the consecration of the new Church of the Saviour, making the fourth Episcopal church, besides nine mission-rooms. The church was in the place of an old and smaller one destroyed in a conflagration which devastated a large part of the city. No less than fourteen clergy, foreign and native, mustered for the occasion. The church is large and handsome, with nave and aisles with granite pillars for the five arches on either side, a good wide chancel and west porch. The native churchwardens and officials met the procession headed by the bishop as we passed from the vestry to the west door, and there read, quite in English fashion, the petition for consecration. Archdeacon Warren preached what was evidently a very powerful sermon, but all the rest of the service, excepting the bishop's part, was taken by the native clergy. The sight was a very impressive one, and then at the Communion none but non-Christians seemed to leave. It was a crammed congregation that remained to communicate.

In the afternoon, whilst I had been addressing the students in the college, my daughter had been occupied in a very touching way. A little girl, twelve years old, a very poor street child who had attended the cottage Sunday school I have described, had been touched and sought instruction for baptism. Her father, a kuruma man, had given his consent, when the child became ill and was sent to hospital. This morning, on our way to church, we received a message that the surgeon had to perform an operation on the child as the only chance of saving life, but she would most probably sink under it. This being told to the girl, she sent at once to say that she must first be baptized. My daughter arranged with Mr. Terasawa to baptize the little convert after the consecration, which he did. In the evening we met a Christian man coming to tell us that the child had died, and the parents wanted a Buddhist funeral. This my daughter could not agree to, as the parents had given their full consent to the child's baptism, and she claimed her as a Christian. We attended the burial the next day, one of the most touching funerals in which I ever joined. The little coffin was covered with a white cloth and a cross of white azaleas upon it, followed by a few Christian women and the heathen parents, whilst a number of kuruma men (her father's comrades) stood crowding round the door, marvelling in the interest that foreigners could take in a poor coolie's child.

Shortly before my departure I had a thoroughly Japanese compliment in a shimbokkwai, the native equivalent of a farewell dinner. Every member of the three Church Missionary Society congregations in Osaka had been invited. The large hall of the school had been cleared and decorated. Singing by the children, speeches—of the purport of which I could only guess until they were interpreted—tea and cakes followed each other in rapid succession. Amongst the speeches I had to make one describing Palestine, and this was interpreted by Mr. Fyson, paragraph by paragraph. Afterwards I had some mysterious drawings sent me on long strips of paper, two of which I found were poems in my honour by a Christian poet of one of the congregations.

As an illustration both of the rapid development of European arts and of mission work, I may mention an expedition which I took with one of our mission ladies, Miss Cox, to a very large match manufactory, employing over a thousand women and girls. This factory was established by a Japanese gentleman who had spent three years in London studying the process as carried on there. These women, who are looked upon as an inferior caste, not only by the makers of artificial flowers, but also by the still lower cotton factory girls, have no instruction whatever; and the proprietor, himself a Buddhist, asked a Buddhist priest to do something for them. He declined, on the ground that the people were too poor to pay for anything. Our missionaries, hearing this, offered their services, which were accepted by the owner, who thought any instruction would be good for them. We had a kuruma ride of some miles to the factory, where we were very courteously received by the owner, who showed us over the works, where everything is done, to the packing in huge cases for transport to India and China, except the cutting and splitting of the wood into the proper size, this being done at another factory. The boxes are made at the people's homes, and is the worst paid occupation in Osaka, but the labels are put on at the factory. Each match passes through fourteen hands, and each operation is carried on in a separate shed. It was a curious sight to see the long rows of women, all nude to the waist, sitting at their work.

A warehouse was placed at Miss Cox's disposal, and at dinner time an announcement made that the foreign lady would like to tell any who were not at work about Christianity. In a minute there was a general rush, the women hastily drawing up their dress over their shoulders, and shouting wildly. We got them to sit down in a semicircle; when Miss Cox, who had hung up a large and brightly coloured picture of the Prodigal Son, began in a ringing voice, and at once there was dead silence and all attention. I counted up to three hundred, when I abandoned the attempt. Of course, I understood not a word that was said; but the proprietor, standing throughout, was evidently pleased and interested, and for three-quarters of an hour the audience remained. The wages of these people range only from threepence to sixpence a day.

Whilst in Osaka I had an opportunity of getting an insight into the necessary accomplishments of a well-bred young lady. First and foremost of these is the art of flower arranging, lessons in which are given in the Bishop Poole Girls' School by a lady, at whose lesson I was once permitted to be present. The same lady also gives lessons there on a very important subject, the mysteries of which I do not pretend to have fathomed, *i.e.*, the proper mode of making and partaking of ceremonial tea. In one of her lectures I was the unfortunate victim operated upon, *i.e.*, I had to act the passive part of the visitor, nis duty being to remain sitting in a posture which to me was by no means restful, and silent for three-quarters of an hour; whilst the hostess, with great dignity, grace and solemnity, brings forward one part of the apparatus after another. With intense exactitude she places each in its appointed spot, passes a carefully folded silk duster over each, and finally ladles hot water on to the tea-powder in the bowl, and this, after being whisked up till it

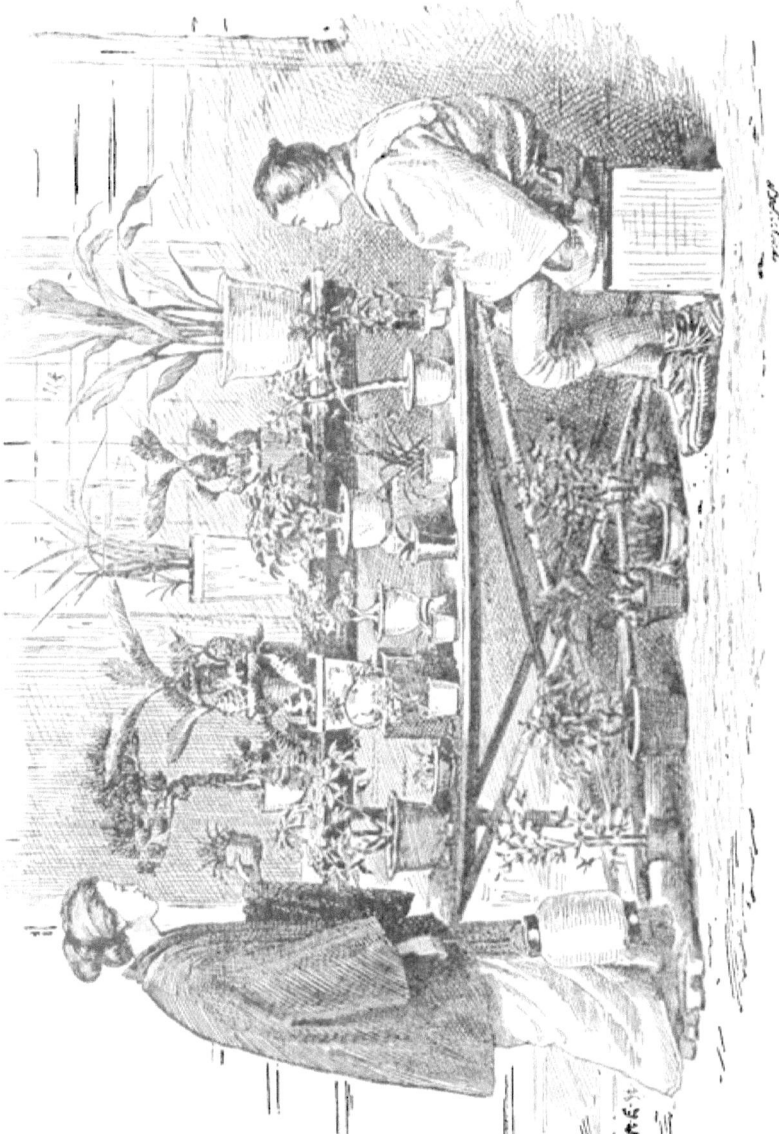

A FLOWER-STAND IN THE STREET. (OSAKA.)

froths, is handed to the visitor, who has to consume it in a specified number of gulps and make no grimaces.

The story of the origin of this strange yet typical ceremony, performed by the daughter at home when it is desired to do special honour to a guest, is as follows :—Some centuries ago, when the country was in a disturbed state, a great statesman, fearing civil war, invented the intricate details of this art of tea-making to compose and calm the minds of the people. So completely did he succeed that all thought of the impending war was soon abandoned, and his fame has come down to posterity as the professor of tea.

When speaking of the lessons in bouquet arrangement I might have described one of the most characteristic sights of Osaka, which I was fortunate enough to witness—the annual spring flower show and fair. It was confined to a certain part of the town, but even so for about a mile flower-pots and plants of every kind seem to have taken the place of all the ordinary wares in the shops, whilst the narrowest passage remained in the centre of the street, lined by stands of flower-pots on either side. There was every variety of horticultural produce, from medallioned chrysanthemums and champion peonies to the humblest ferns from the woods, and potsherds containing the root of some wild flower beseechingly offered for a few rin by the most squalid of the poor. It seemed to be the one opportunity for many a poor outcast to earn an honest farthing. It was impossible to resist the silent appeals, far more successful than the noisy importunities of an Arab bazaar. The purchasing mania was irresistible, and we hired one kuruma after another to carry home our floral purchases, having invested in a whole forest of dwarfed pines, maples, and oranges, the largest of which could be covered by a hat. The most curious thing of all was a large shallow flower-pot containing what might be called a doll-house garden, but all of actually living plants, with little walks, and microscopic mountains and lakes, the latter spanned by bridges, and the former with houses perched about them.

CHAPTER VIII

SHIKOKU

NOT the least interesting expedition which we made from Osaka was one to the neighbouring island of Shikoku, an island which even yet is very rarely visited by foreigners, excepting those connected with the few mission stations. It is in area the fourth of the great islands which constitute the empire, and may be called the Wales of Japan, and the island of Awaji, an intermediate link with the main island, suggests the Isle of Man. In its physical aspect, too, its bold mountainous character reminds one of Wales, while in the south part of the island there is a dense population, rich mines, and extensive manufactures. It is divided into four provinces, or as a Japanese geographer has expressed it, 'It has one body and four faces, and each face has a name.' Quaint indeed are these names, their literal translation being 'Lovely Princess,' 'Prince Good-boiled-rice,' 'Princess of Great-food,' and 'Brave Good-youth.' The people of Shikoku, and especially of the south, have always been reputed to be the most turbulent and democratic, which is probably explained by their employments being largely mining and manufacturing. In this part of the country the American Presbyterian Mission has been at work for some years. The result may be judged of by the fact that this island has returned several Christians to the Japanese Parliament, and among them was the Speaker of the first House of Commons.

Our voyage from Osaka to Tokushima in this island, though not long, was certainly amusing, the accommodation and arrangements being purely Japanese. The voyage being in an almost entirely land-locked sea, the boat was constructed rather after the model of a river steamer than of an ocean-going boat, and, with due consideration to the economising of the passengers' time, was made at night. Soon after sunset, preceded by a boy with a barrow and lantern, we went down to the wharf, from which we entered the steamer through a hole in her side, and then up a ladder on to the deck. But the deck was only a space of two feet all round the ship, the centre being occupied by the third-class cabin, which was just five feet high, being intended for sitting and sleeping in, certainly not for walking. There being no berths, 'first come, first served,' was the rule, and the passengers as they arrived promptly secured quarters for the night by spreading a red blanket and disposing their persons thereupon. Into this we had to go on all-fours, creep across it while the passengers were lying thick, and get down another ladder to the second-class cabin, which occupied the whole width of the vessel. Taking off our shoes, we could, stooping, walk along it into the first-class cabin, of the same width, with plenty of port-holes open for air, and a fixed bench along each side. The floor was carpeted over the mats, and two or three feeble oil lamps suspended were just enough to make darkness visible. The circumambient bench, which I had erroneously imagined to be berths, proved to be only the receptacle intended for baggage. However, spreading my rug, I made myself comfortable on the bench, with my head close to an open port-hole. Happily there were only two passengers besides

LADY MISSIONARIES' HOUSE.

ourselves, both Japanese gentlemen, and we had abundant space in a cabin supposed to accommodate twenty of both sexes. With the full complement, sardines in a box would have been a fitting comparison. For an hour or two tea was continually being served, pipes smoked, and conversation was ceaseless; while my daughter, more acclimatised than myself, sat country fashion on the floor with her writing board on her knees. Quaint and novel as was my bedchamber, I had a fairly good night's rest, though I could not but regret that we were losing some of the most charming scenery, equal to that of the Inland Sea, as we coasted down the west side of the island of Awaji. At 4.30 A.M. we were roused to go and wash in turns outside, before the second class; according to the due precedence of first-class passengers. My toilet completed, I clambered on to the top of the third-class cabin, and had a lovely view of the labyrinth of islets, all well wooded, through which we were winding. For the last hour we steamed up a wide sluggish river till we reached Tokushima, and before landing were supplied with a Japanese breakfast on the floor. All the other passengers, being natives, had been allowed to land at once, but we had to wait until the police functionary, not an early riser, could condescend to come on board and examine our passports. This formality over, we drove across the city to the house of Mr. Buncombe, of the Church Missionary Society, our kind host. With 61,000 inhabitants, it is the tenth city in Japan, while the island has nearly 4,000,000. The second city, Kochi, is rather further off than Cork is from Belfast, and though less populous than Tokushima, is more important for its manufactures, and has a well-manned American Presbyterian Mission.

Mr. Buncombe had been out in Japan four years, and was the first missionary ever stationed here, but the church had been gradually growing up for some years before his arrival, and had been visited from

the Osaka Mission. There is a church and native parsonage with an ordained native pastor, partly supported by the people, and two preaching-rooms in different parts of the city, which I visited, with two native catechists at work, besides one itinerating in the surrounding villages. Two lady missionaries had also recently arrived, and were settled in a pretty little Japanese cottage not far from the mission station.

There is not much of striking interest in Tokushima, with its long straight streets running in parallel lines for a mile or two. In the centre is a rocky mound, surrounded by a moat, and covered with noble trees, now the Park, formerly the Daimio's Castle, but now entirely dismantled. Overhanging the city is a precipitous wooded hill, with a fine Shinto temple on its brow. To this we climbed—not a very arduous task, as steps have been cut in the side of the cliff, and were richly rewarded by a superb panorama. The mingling of sea and land, of mountain, forest, and plain, was an epitome of Japanese scenery. In front of us was spread out the city, beyond it the bay, covered with fishing-boats, into which two rivers flow from different points; one of them, the Yoshi-no-gawa, navigable for many miles, while on both sides mountain ranges tower to some height, clad with dark pine forest, and their sides frequently pierced with the pale green patches which marked the openings of the rich cultivated valleys. To the right, across the principal river, on the distant plain, a dark brown patch examined under a field glass would reveal a large town, in the centre of cultivated fields, and beyond that again a dim grey line of mountain heights.

In the afternoon we called upon the native clergyman, Mr. Terata, and his wife, who speak a little English. He is considered the most able of the native clergy and the most eloquent preacher, and is very obnoxious to the Buddhists. His life has often been threatened, but he seemed to be outliving the persecutions. In one church or other there are

MISSIONARY'S HOUSE AT TOKUSHIMA.

lectures or services every night, conducted by Mr. Buncombe, Mr. Terata, or a catechist. In the largest mission church which we visited was an outer porch, with pigeon-holes on either side from top to bottom, where the members of the congregation might deposit their shoes or sandals. There was also a stock of new fans, for the summer was coming on, and these are provided for the comfort of the worshippers. The

Japanese are as ingenious and enterprising in advertising as any pushing tradesman at home. At a church council meeting a member of the congregation offered to present 200 fans as a gift. He is a photographer, and produced a sample of his fans, but one side was covered with an elaborate advertisement of his establishment. As a contemplation of the attractions of his studio would hardly have conduced to the

MISSION-ROOM, TOKUSHIMA.

devotion of the worshippers, Mr. Buncombe suggested a more appropriate embellishment, and to the credit of the enterprising advertiser be it said, he adopted the design and supplied the fans. Most appropriate it was; on one side was a coloured sketch of a stormy sea, with a dark, lowering sky, and the passage, 'Jesus Christ came into the world to save sinners.' On the reverse was depicted a brilliant sunlit sky, with a wooded islet in a calm sea, and storks flying overhead, and the text, 'God is a Spirit, and they that worship Him must worship Him in spirit and in truth.'

In the evening, beginning at six o'clock, there was a grand shimbokkwai, or entertainment, held in the mission-room out of compliment to the visitors. It was rather a formidable affair, and as full of formalities as ceremonial tea. The room was absolutely devoid of furniture, and the guests as they arrived ranged themselves round the walls, sitting on their heels. Between forty and fifty came, all, of course, church members, the majority being men; and the few women ranged themselves against the wall opposite to the men. I stood near the door, and was formally introduced to each visitor separately. I had consequently much practice in bowing twice to each one till my head touched my knees. The same ceremonial was repeated by each new-comer to the previous arrivals round the walls. I was much taken with the appearance of one member, a stout old farmer from the neighbourhood, the treasurer of the Nippon Sei-ko-kwai, or Japan church of the district. He arrived on horseback, and his horse, one of the few really thoroughbreds that I ever saw in the country, was turned out to graze in the adjoining yard. I found that I won the thorough approval of my friend by appreciating the points of his steed. When all had arrived, after a few minutes' solemn silence, Mr. Terata stood up and made a short speech, and was followed by others, of the purport of all which I knew nothing. Mr. Buncombe gave them what I believe was supposed to be my history, after which I was expected duly to respond, and did so in English, one of the company volunteering to translate for me, sentence by sentence. This over, the churchwardens brought in saucer plates and paper napkins with pictures on them for each guest. Then tea was served, and a large paper bag of sweet cakes of all colours and shapes was set before each guest. Each took a little and wrapped up the remainder, first in paper and then in a handkerchief, to take away with them. It would have been a gross breach of etiquette if we had not done the same. To me the entertainment, with the conversation going on in an undertone among the guests, seemed rather like a Scotch funeral. At length, about nine o'clock, we made our round of bows to everyone, gave our apologies in correct style for going first, and with many a 'sayonara,' or goodbye, departed, though the entertainment continued till near midnight. To me a shimbokkwai is the acme of dulness, but then it must be remembered that I understood not a word, unlike my friends, who had a bright remark for everyone.

One day was spent in a delightful expedition along the coast to Muya, a large straggling town twelve miles off, an out-station of the mission, and to the celebrated Straits of Naruto. A party of six, we started each in a kuruma drawn by two men, pulling tandem. It was a lovely ride. The road was level, on a narrow plain, with a wooded mountain range on our left and the islet-studded sea on the right. The plain itself was covered chiefly with barley, just

S

assuming its ripening golden-coloured hue, and many villages with picturesque little temples, Shinto and Buddhist, with avenues of trees leading up to them. May they soon become village churches! We crossed five rivers, some of considerable width, and alive with boats. Two of them were spanned by pontoon bridges, one of which is two-thirds of a mile long, and is washed away every year, in consequence of which a toll of three sen (1½d.) is charged to all passengers. If kuruma-riding were not so solitary it would have been the perfection of an outing.

After halting at the mission-house and being introduced to the catechist, who had been at college, and hoped soon to be ordained, we went on to a native inn fronting the sea, in a lovely cove with rocky islets crowding in front, surmounted by pine-trees. How these trees can live and get nourishment apparently on the top of a naked rock I do not pretend to understand. Their roots seem to bind the rocks and penetrate to the water's edge. After dining Japanese fashion on the floor, we crossed a creek in a boat, when most of the party landed and had a three-miles walk to Naruto. As we walked along the strand, strewn with shells, many of them most gorgeous olives, cowries, and cones, I could have wished for a long day, simply to explore these sands. It was a lively scene. Every three hundred yards fishermen with their boats were hauling in their nets, and scores of women and children in wild excitement were tugging at them and seizing the struggling fish. The line of nets taken out by each boat in a semicircle

almost touched one another for miles along the coast, and though being constantly drawn in, very few were ever drawn empty. The inhabitants of the sea must indeed swarm among these islands. Nor were these draw-nets the only mode of gathering in the harvest of the sea. Many a small bamboo buoy marked the lobster-pots or eel-traps to arrest the unwary among these still waters, while in boats further out we could see the fishermen hauling in their small-meshed nets with great catches of sardines, and others patiently dropping their long lines with bait. No fish appears to be rejected as unclean, for two or three species of dog-fish seem very common, and are much appreciated in the market. The favourite fish is one called tai, a species of *serranus*, or sea-perch. So much is it appreciated that the proverb has arisen, 'Tai, even if it is bad, still it is tai.'

At the further end of this little bay a bold wooded bluff projects into the sea, to the summit of which was a well-trodden path. From the platform at the top, disfigured by the papers of Japanese picnic parties, we had a lovely view of the opening of the Inland Sea and its countless islets. Descending on the other side, after gathering a dozen species of ferns I had never before seen, we found ourselves at Naruto, one of the lions of Japan. Here the tide coming up the Inland Sea meets the tide from the north. It must be remembered that the island of Awaji lies right across a wide bay of this sea from the main island to the northern point of Shikoku, leaving a channel of considerable width to the northward, which is the commercial route to Kobe and Osaka; and more than thirty miles south of it, at the other extremity of Awaji, is the narrow channel of Naruto, interrupted by several islets, and therefore of little commercial importance. Its narrowest part is about a mile and a quarter wide, but a rocky island divides the strait into what are called the Greater and Lesser Naruto, the Greater Naruto being on the Shikoku side. We must remember that the tidal wave, rolling from west to east, strikes the north and south entrances of the Inland Sea almost simultaneously; but Naruto being near the northern opening, the tidal wave reaches this narrow channel from the north long before the arrival of the southern wave. The consequence is that at high water from the north, the sea is twelve feet higher on the northern side of the channel than it is on the inside, by a sort of bore being arrested here, but at low water the conditions are reversed, and the tidal wave having now come up from the south, the water north of the strait is twelve feet lower at an ordinary spring tide. The consequence is that there is literally a waterfall across the sea, excepting for a few minutes at mid-tide, when it is level. We were fortunate enough to arrive just at high water. A small reef only two or three feet above high water-mark runs out into the sea exactly in a line with the waterfall. We could easily walk out on to it, and there, standing on a flat rock at the extremity, the sea on our right hand was several feet higher than on our left, and the line in front of us

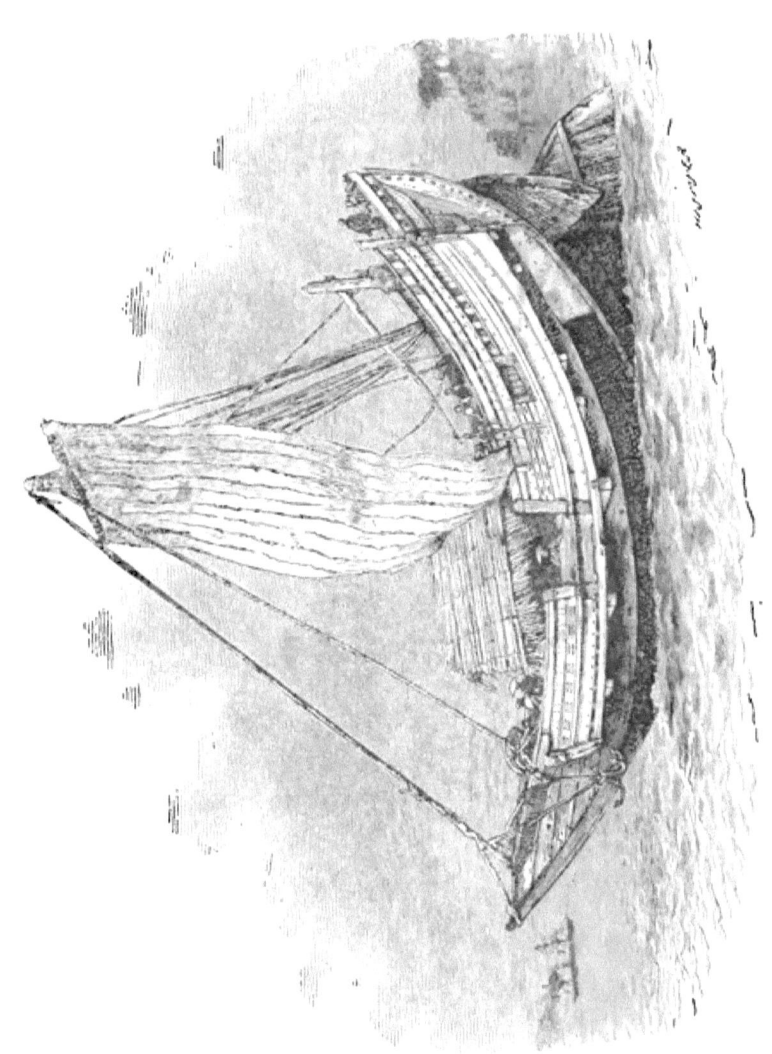

was an even cascade more than a mile long, and as we watched it the waterfall gradually diminished in height. We went on shore, and after spending an hour or two botanising in the woods, returned to our post of observation to find the cascade barely more than a foot in height. Large shipping dare not risk this dangerous passage, but lighter craft can easily shoot the falls either way. We watched two junks trying it. They were gradually drawn faster and faster, as the current bore them down, till at last they ducked to it, seemed to take a header, and instantly come up again, and were then swept down stream at a tremendous rate. I have shot the rapids in the St. Lawrence, but none of them were like this. Unfortunately time did not permit us to remain to see the water perfectly even, as it is for a few minutes before it begins to rise on the other side. As it was, it was far into the night before we reached Tokushima again.

I left the island of Shikoku with the conviction that there is no part of the Japanese empire which would so well repay a leisurely exploration of a few weeks as would Shikoku. Though the mountain ranges are far inferior in elevation to those of the mainland, yet they are more densely and uniformly wooded. The population of the island, although reaching 4,000,000, is not so evenly dispersed as elsewhere, and consequently the extent of primeval forest is much greater. Game, and especially deer, must be very plentiful, judging by the abundance of heads and horns to be seen everywhere, though I only noticed one species, *Cervus sika*, or one closely allied to it.

CHAPTER IX

THE ISLAND OF KIUSHIU

VERY different from our passage-boat to Tokushima was the sumptuous passenger steamer on which, a few days after our return from Shikoku, we embarked to pass again down the lovely Inland Sea, up which I had sailed a few weeks before. Our object was to visit the northern and central portions of the island of Kiushiu. By a most convenient arrangement the passengers were expected to be all on board the Saikyo Maru in the evening, so that we could loose from our moorings at daybreak, and lost none of the scenery. In the most perfect of weather we steamed down the Inland Sea, amidst a prospect simply peerless for calm, rich, quiet beauty. All that sunlight, a silver sea, countless islets on both sides, mountains clad with timber from the shore to their summits, villages in rapid succession, some half buried in woods, others fringing the shore, innumerable fishing-boats and junks, amidst which the steamer carefully threads her way—all that these can give of beauty are here. Not majestic or grand, but delicately, gracefully, sweetly beautiful.

We were reminded that sometimes there is a reverse to the medal, when during the afternoon we passed the wreck of a large English steamer, which had gone ashore on an islet eight days ago, and was now lying on her side, a hopeless wreck, since there was no available machinery within reach to raise her. Amongst our fellow-passengers was the ubiquitous Lloyd's agent, whom we dropped in a gig on his mission to look after the salvage, and many were the condolences he received on his departure for the Robinson Crusoe's island, where he would probably have to remain a fortnight alone amongst the fishermen. He was, however, well furnished with provisions, and light literature for solitary hours was showered upon him as he left the vessel.

The sun did not set until we had reached that part of the Inland Sea the prospect of which I had enjoyed in daylight on my former voyage. We were due at the Straits of Shimanoseki in the early morning hours, and here the steamer was to drop anchor until daylight, this being her only point of call on her way to Shanghai. The night was too bright to allow me to leave the deck, where I could mark the clear dark outline of mountains and islands over the phosphorescent sea, and that with most agreeable companions. The captain, a cultured American, who had kept his eyes open all over the world, and the chief engineer, an observant Scotchman, who had spent years in Yezo as his headquarters, and took a deep interest in the Ainu aborigines, kept the watch. The engineer was a devoted admirer of Mr. Batchelor, the Church Missionary Society missionary to the Ainu in Yezo, and it was refreshing to hear his high opinion of the missionary staff and of their work in Japan.

About 2.30 A.M. we anchored in the narrow strait of Shimanoseki, which locks the south-west entrance of the Inland Sea. To the north, on the main island, is Bakan, well defended by earthworks, and Mōji, our point of departure in Kiushiu, on the other side. We remained on board till dawn, when we were supplied with coffee and landed in the ship's boat at Mōji. A portion of the North Kiushiu Railway had just been opened, but the station was not yet completed; and finding ourselves an hour before the time of starting, we deposited our luggage on the planks and set out to explore the village in search of food, not very successfully. A journey of three hours through a rich undulating country brought us to Hakata. The line generally skirted the seashore.

We passed Kokura, a bustling seaport garrison town, and after that a number of collieries, recently opened, for this is the northern extension of the great Kiushiu coal-field, which extends eighty miles southward. A Japanese company is making arrangements for an enormous development of these coal-mines, which have hitherto been chiefly worked only by drifts. The upper seam alone has as yet been worked at all, but shafts have here been sunk, and several lower seams have been reached, yielding steam coal of the best quality. The Japanese fully expect to monopolize the coal trade of the Eastern Pacific, as the seams can be worked close to some of the best harbours, whilst the abundance of labour and its low price will enable them to compete successfully, not only with England, but with Vancouver. As yet coal hardly can be considered an article of household consumption in Japan, its home use being entirely confined to manufactures. The natives as yet show no disposition to apply it to domestic purposes, and prefer the more costly wood charcoal, which is a much less dangerous fuel in their inflammable wooden houses, while their paper walls and many chinks remove all danger of asphyxia. Still, it is to be hoped that mineral coal will be adopted for domestic purposes before the forests of the country, to which it owes so much, not only of its beauty, but its fertility, be too much depleted. To this last-mentioned danger, however, the enlightened government seems to be already alive, and sets an example which we might well follow at home, by locking the door before the steed is stolen. In India we have been barely in time to arrest the mischief which the denudation of timber has already caused in the desolation of more than one of the West Indian Islands, and which there are ominous signs may ere long overtake great parts of the North American continent. In Japan the government is following the German method of systematic replanting.

We left the railway at Hakata, a large town separated from Fukuoka, our destination, only by the Nakagawa or Middle River, spanned by bridges. We rode through both towns to the hospitable house of our host, Mr. Hind, who, with Mr. Hutchinson, represents the Church Missionary Society in this great town and district. Fukuoka itself has a population of 53,000, and is a military centre, as in case of war, whether with China or Russia, the Straits of Shimanoseki would be a vital point either to hold or to attack. The far-seeing policy of the government has massed, in the different old castles and barracks within striking distance of the Straits, a number of skeleton corps which can easily be filled up. Fukuoka, though not much talked of, contains really many objects of interest. Very soon after our arrival Mr. Hind took us to the top of a hill at the extremity of the city, whence we had a commanding view of the bay and of the crescent-shaped city fringing it for four miles. The sea with its boats and shipping looked almost as populous as the land. Though flourishing and beautifully clean, the streets are rather too modern to be very attractive, excepting for their shops, which are well supplied, and in which I was able to pick up some interesting genuine old bronzes.

The palace and grounds of the old Daimios skirt the further side of the city, and contain many objects of interest. The public park, which is formed out of a part of the ancient Daimios' domain, is studded with noble pine-trees, extending to the shore. Adjoining it is the mausoleum of the old Princes of Chikusen, quite unique in Japan, and unlike anything I ever saw elsewhere. Like the park, it is full of magnificent pine-trees, towering above the maples and other trees, which they overshadow. Among these forming a labyrinth are dropped the megalithic monuments of the family, sometimes placed on artificial mounds, sometimes encircled with evergreen-trees, and sometimes on the summit of a taller mound reached by a flight of steps. The tombs of the male members of the family have square shafts on circular bases, and are of great size and covered with old Chinese characters. Those of the females have circular shafts.

This family, one of the most powerful in former times, next to the Shogun, has played a conspicuous part in the history of Japan. They were the leaders of the Christian faction in the time of Spanish influence. The Daimio Kuroda Nagamasa, in A.D. 1623, is frequently mentioned in the Jesuit chronicles. The inscription on his tomb is very long, and the tomb itself consists of three truncated columns placed one above the other, each on a circular base. A massive pagoda roof shelters it, giving it very much the appearance of a temple. I much regretted I could not read the inscription, nor ascertain what his Buddhist descendants have said about his Christianity. The grounds are kept strictly private, and are in beautiful order. We were only admitted by special favour, and enjoyed wandering in the maze of thickets till sunset. The family is one of the few who have retained considerable political influence in new Japan, and the last Daimio of the Kuroda family has been created an hereditary marquis. His eldest son is a graduate of Oxford, but, instead of following the traditions of the family history, is a prominent anti-foreigner and anti-Christian.

I cannot leave Fukuoka without a word on the infant church in that district, where we spent two Sundays, and on the second had the almost unique privilege of assisting in the formal consecration of a native church, built almost entirely by the people. I was especially struck by the two catechists whom I met, and one of whom has been since ordained. His history is interesting. By birth a gentleman, he was originally a Samurai or retainer of the Satsuma clan. After the abolition of the feudal system, he received as compensation a sum of about $400. He was then a schoolmaster. Hearing something of Christianity, he became so much interested in it that he resigned his post and went with his family to Nagasaki, where he sought instruction from Archdeacon Maundrell, and was ultimately baptized. He then entered the little college there, at his own charges, to be trained as a catechist. He never said a word about his means, but lived on his capital till it was exhausted, and it was only when he was utterly penniless that the fact came out. He has proved himself an admirable man, and it was understood that he was to be ordained as soon as the congregation were able to guarantee their part of his stipend.

The other catechist, who works the neighbouring out-stations, was a bank clerk. Having accidentally heard a catechist, he was led to seek further instruction, and on his baptism was dismissed from the bank for having become a Christian. He was in absolute destitution for a time, but refused all help from Christian friends, lest it should be said he had gone over for what he could get. He was reduced to support his family by cleaning out and taking care of the government schools. Mr. Hutchinson, however, soon found out his position, and, as he was a man of education and a gentleman, was able at once to employ him as a catechist, in which post he is invaluable. It is interesting to know that the manager of the bank where he once was is now a trustee and churchwarden of the native church.

Another case worth mentioning is that of Mr. Hutchinson's cook. He was a strong Buddhist, and was keeper of the Sailors' Home at Nagasaki. He was led to think that there must be something in Christianity by noticing the lives of some of the sailors there, whom he observed to gather in a corner for reading and prayer. He argued there must be something in this that made these men so different from the others, and therefore, to get instruction, came and offered himself to Mr. Hutchinson as his servant, and insisted upon accompanying him when he moved from Nagasaki. He has been the means of bringing all his kinsfolk into the Christian fold.

I was also introduced to the oldest Christian in the congregation, and one of the most earnest. He is a blind man, who gets his living by hawking halfpenny newspapers in the street. He is called the father of the new church, because about two years ago he said at a prayer meeting: 'We ought not to be content to worship in a hired house; we ought to build ourselves a church. I will undertake to give $30 in two years for the purpose. What will others give?' This was indeed an enormous sum in a country where a working man earns $3 a month. A shopkeeper exclaimed: 'If he can give $30, I must give $50;' and others followed suit. So $800 was raised, and the church was built.

We were at the last service held in the old mission-room—a hired house of two stories, the lower of which, open to the street, was devoted to preaching to the heathen, and for holding various inquirers' meetings, while the upper chamber was the church in which Christians met for worship. It might possibly hold a hundred people seated close together on the floor. I found the crowd and heat overpowering, and fear I did not set an example of attention, but I may be excused. I wonder if my reader ever tried to listen to an unknown tongue for two hours while sitting on the floor in a cramped posture. If so, I am sure I shall be forgiven.

The following Sunday was a day much to be remembered in the history of the infant church of Kiushiu. Bishop Bickersteth had arrived the previous evening for the consecration of the new church, which by working night and day was completed—a feat that seemed hopeless a few days before. The matting was all down, the seats up (for they determined to have seats in their new church, a foreign fashion which is creeping in), the windows were all in, as the procession, consisting of the church committee, catechists from town and country, three clergy and the bishop, entered and walked up the church.

There was a crowd, as there would be elsewhere on such an occasion. Many non-Christians were present, among them several officials from the Kenchō (government offices), and some leading merchants. The men were on one side, the women on the other, but soon the men overflowed into the ladies' seats. Almost all the men were got up in European fashion, frock coats predominating; but I was glad to notice that there was not a single female, whether of higher or lower rank, in Western costume; nor did I ever during my wanderings meet a woman in any but the national dress. We can only hope that, warned by the mean appearance of the other sex in the unbecoming habiliments that it is fashionable to adopt, the ladies' style will never change.

The ceremonial seemed to be exactly as at home: the petition for consecration, the lawyer's part, and the handing and signing of title and trust deeds, were all duly performed at the communion table. After the consecration was a confirmation of eight adult men and three women converts, and the Holy Communion, with sixty-four communicants besides the clergy. The people are fond of sermons, and at the evening service after the bishop's address and confirmation there were two sermons to a crowded congregation, preached by catechists, the second being of portentous length from a young man gifted with Hibernian eloquence and more than Hibernian vehemence.

While speaking of the consecration, I forgot to mention the ceremonial connected with the building, which is exactly the reverse of the Western custom. We lay foundation stones. In this country, on the contrary, buildings are always begun by setting up the roof-tree and then completing the whole roof supported by a wooden pillar at each angle, from which they build the wooden walls downwards, having a shelter under which to work. As soon as the ridge of the roof is fixed, and before the rafters have been attached to it, in the centre of the beam a hole is cut, in which the bottle of documents and coins are deposited with as much ceremony as amongst ourselves. When I first noticed this amusing contrast to our ancient Western custom, I was naturally led to associate it with the fact that no trace whatever of Freemasonry has been found in Japan, where the building material being exclusively wood and not stone, there was no scope for those operative masonic traditions which are so interwoven with speculative Freemasonry.

The situation of the church is certainly the choicest in Fukuoka, adjoining the large Post Office buildings, facing the river, with the wide roadway of the quay in front, lined with barges and sampans, and close to the bridge which unites the two towns. The porch has granite pillars, and is at the south-west angle of the building, surmounted, as are also the east and west gables, with the cross in a circle. The fine granite font was the gift of two members of the congregation.

Early on the Monday morning we proceeded on our way by rail to the station for Dazaifu, one of the interesting historical sites in the island. Having deposited our luggage, we took kurumas across the plain to the foot of the hills where Dazaifu is situated, a most interesting old place, the seat of the government of Kiushiu two thousand years ago and more. The island used to be a dependency, only nominally subject to the Mikado, who appointed the governor-general, and was not really incorporated in the empire until A.D. 1338. The temples here are the most ancient in Japan. One of them is dedicated to Tenjin (*i.e.*, heaven man), the name under which a great ruler and scholar, Sugawara, has been deified. In his day, 900 A.D., the governorship of Kiushiu was looked upon as a banishment and disgrace. It was the post to which illustrious or powerful men who might have offended the Mikado were relegated. Tenjin is worshipped as the god of caligraphy. In front of the temples dedicated to his honour is generally placed the figure of a recumbent cow, in accordance with the tradition that, having no horses in his exile, he used to ride about on a cow. His temple at Dazaifu is approached by a long avenue and a torii (*i.e.*, gateway) of bronze, of a size such as I saw nowhere else. The avenue was flanked by splendid bronze statues of dragons, lions and cows, larger than life-size, and some of the finest camphor-trees I ever saw.

The temple itself was more striking from the evidences of its antiquity than its beauty, and in the courtyard in front of it were again many bronze figures of cows, lions and owls. The priests were much pleased for a fee to show us the relics and treasures of this temple, the swords of many historical characters by famous makers, some a thousand years old, manuscripts claiming to be fifteen hundred years old, the original holographs of one of the greatest poets of Japan, bronze statuettes of Confucius and his chief followers, brought from China in 630 A.D., and many choice specimens of ancient lacquer. In fact, the sacrarium of this temple was simply the treasure-house of an antiquarian and historical museum.

We walked on a mile or so further to visit a still older temple, somewhat dilapidated, but with yet older relics than the other, amongst them the metal mirror of the first Emperor of Japan, B.C. ?, of unknown date, and some ancient lacquer work. It was an exercise of patience to wait for the exhibition of the historic swords, which had more wrappings and cases than the mummy of an Egyptian monarch. Seating himself on the ground after opening one coffer and then another, the priest would take out the long package, enfolded in marvellous wrappers of faded silk embroidery, tied with broad ribbons in knots which seemed to have some mystic meaning, and it was not until after some half-dozen of these covertures had been successively unfolded that the sword in its elaborately inlaid sheath was revealed.

The temple of Kwannon, the goddess of mercy, not far off, was well worth a visit, as it also possesses a number of interesting relics. In the centre of the building is a colossal figure of Kwannon, with two other smaller yet colossal statues on either side, all three gilt, or rather, if the priest's statement be true, covered with thin gold plates. If so, they must be of fabulous value. A walk of two miles more took us to the site of the old court-house and palace of Dazaifu. Little now remains of the old capital of the island except the granite bases of the columns of the building, and the colonnade leading to it, but its shape and outline can be clearly traced. It reminded us on approaching it of a Druidical circlet.

We had a hurried walk down to the nearest village, where we were able to hire kurumas, and caught the last train towards Kumamoto, our bourne. The line was not yet opened, and the train deposited us fifteen miles short of our destination. When we reached the terminus—it could hardly be called a station—no kuruma man was willing to take us on, as it was too far and too late. However, we persuaded some at last to convey us at least to the first village. Here we were set down in the road in front of a tea-house, and certainly the poor fellows who had brought us deserved their fare, and were quite incapable of going further, for when we engaged them they were, so to speak, return empties, having done their day's work. There seemed no help for it, so we sat down on a mat in the tea-house, resigned, if necessary, to spend the night there, and made a meal as best we could of tea and sugared beans. At length two villagers, seeing the chances of a stiff fare, presented themselves and agreed to take us on.

It was a pity to lose the rich scenery, but we had time before sunset to halt for a visit to the fine monument erected on a mound of the battlefield where the Satsuma rebellion was finally crushed. This was, in fact, the Culloden of Japan, the last struggle of the clans and feudal independence against centralised government and the new *régime*. It had lasted for several years, and was finally crushed in 1877.

Our friends Mr. and Mrs. Brandram, of the Church Missionary Society at Kumamoto, had almost given us up in despair when at length our kuruma men found their house. We found, besides the family party, a young Japanese doctor who spoke English perfectly. By a strange coincidence this gentleman, who was a complete stranger passing through Kumamoto on his way to a distant town, had called on Mr. Brandram as a fellow-Christian. In the course of conversation, my daughter's name being mentioned, he said that he had been invited to my house in England and knew some of my friends. Not a little astonished was he when told that we were expected that very evening, and he agreed to stay to meet us. Strange that in this remote town in Japan three of us should meet who had never seen each other before, and yet had many common tangents—Dr. Saiki being an Edinburgh graduate well known to my friends, Mr. Brandram the curate of an old curate, and Mrs. Brandram the daughter of an old friend.

Kumamoto, with its population of 60,000, is the most important military centre in Kiushiu. This it owes chiefly to the very commanding position of its

ancient fortress, which is equally important under the conditions of modern warfare. Like the Castle of Nagoya, it has happily escaped the ravages of the iconoclastic fever of twenty years ago, and next to it is perhaps the finest relic of the feudal times. I may best describe it as an inland Gibraltar, standing on a rock, precipitous and unassailable on three sides, and commanding not only the whole town beneath, but the surrounding country. It is now to Kiushiu what Osaka is to the main island, the artillery depôt of the country, and admission to the fortress is strictly forbidden except under special circumstances. I was fortunate enough to see the horse artillery practice on a field day; and although the horses did not seem comparable in breeding to our own, yet I am quite sure that the rapidity with which the evolutions were gone through, the promptitude with which the guns were limbered and unlimbered, would not have discredited the best European troops.

This wonderful castle was built by the Kato, conqueror of Korea, nearly four hundred years ago, but is chiefly celebrated now for the spirited defence which its small garrison made in 1877 against the Satsuma insurgents, led by their hero Saigo. He was the champion of the old system, and though he had been foremost in assisting to abolish the Shogunate and draw forth the Mikado into real authority, yet he was determinately opposed to all the modern innovations, more perhaps to the abolition of feudalism than to the recognition of foreigners. He had rallied about twenty thousand young Samurai of the class to whom the new institutions meant ruin, and so unprepared were the central authorities then for resistance, that, probably, had he marched straight to Tokio, he would have carried all before him. His one and fatal mistake was that, instead of being content with masking Kumamoto, he wasted weeks in attempting to reduce it by siege, and thus gave the government time to collect their forces at Fukuoka. The siege being raised, the gallant Saigo, after several struggles being finally defeated, when all was lost at Kagoshima, got a friend to decapitate him, and thus terminated the last effort of old Japan.

The mausoleum of the old Daimios is full of interest, though on a much smaller scale than the one at Fukuoka. One of the Daimios in A.D. 1600 was a well-known Christian, but his descendants have given him a Buddhist epitaph on his tomb. The gardens of this old family are now the public park of the place, quaint and artificial, with lakes and mounds, and the azaleas just past their full beauty. The town has one feature not common in Japan, that all the streets are more like boulevards, from the rows of trees planted down them. Almost the whole city having been burnt at the time of the siege, opportunity was taken to treat the place as was old London after its great fire. Kumamoto is an important educational centre, with a large government college and very extensive buildings. The Professor of English, a Canadian fellow-countryman, who has since left, most kindly showed us over everything, and especially the museum, where I picked up some information, though I was sorry to find that the authorities had not yet learned the importance of noting the localities of their specimens.

One evening during our stay we attended a shimbokkwai given in the town hall, and attended by nearly three hundred Christians, in honour of a native catechist of the Church Missionary Society, who was leaving on account of health. The Church Missionary Society is by no means the only mission in this great city, and the interesting feature about the affair is that it was got up by the Christians of other denominations as a brotherly farewell.

CHAPTER X

ASO SAN AND THE GEYSERS OF YUNOTAN

FROM Kumamoto we made an intensely interesting two days' excursion to Aso San, an active volcano, 5,900 feet above the sea, almost exactly in the centre of the island. Aso San is the second or third in importance of the fifty-one volcanoes which are reckoned in the country, and it has, moreover, many satellites in the form of sulphur jets, hot springs, and magnificent geysers. It is never at rest, though at present it was not ejecting anything beyond sulphur and smoke. The last eruption of consequence was in February, 1884, when there was no stream of lava, but showers of ashes fell, and destroyed the crops within a radius of thirty miles, and at Kumamoto the darkness continued for three days. It was also active, but not to the same extent, in 1889, simultaneously with the Kumamoto earthquake.

We organised a party of six for the expedition, three ladies, Mr. Lang, of the Church Missionary Society, and Mr. Brandram's Japanese servant, who, knowing the district well, proved himself an invaluable dragoman. After an early start we rode for five hours in kurumas, each in solitary state, choosing for the sake of the scenery, in preference to the new and lower road, the old Ozu road, under an avenue of pine-trees 300 years old. Our journey was through a rich cultivated country, gently rising, the pine and cryptomeria avenues giving grateful shade, every now and then interrupted by picturesque villages, with the women busily threshing wheat and barley by the roadside with flails on great mats, the men toiling in the paddy fields, whence the barley had been cleared. After this, the earliest harvest of the year, not a moment is lost; the water is turned in by the little channels which intersect the plain in every direction, and form a perfect network of parallelograms, fed by the mountain rills, and led in this direction or in that with perfect docility, as the little mud walls of the channel are opened or closed. Here the parties of husbandmen in long rows were busy dibbling in the young rice plants in the black semi-fluid mud. In other fields men were busily pulling up by the roots the long rows of wheat plants, which had all been drilled in, for the Japanese agriculturist would scorn the slovenly and wasteful method of sowing broadcast, and as the wheat was uprooted, long rows of indigo or lentils sown between the drills were briskly shooting up, now that they had space and light for growth. The plain on either side stretched far as the eye could reach, dotted all over with labourers in their large bamboo umbrella hats, a perfect picture of agricultural peace and prosperity.

We gradually approached what seemed a mighty convex wall of mountain, in which just before us a solitary deep gap was cleft, up to which a mighty causeway led by a gentle slope from the plain. Here at a tea-house we dismissed our kuruma men, and secured two porters for our hand luggage. We were gradually entering the one gap in the great circular crater of the most stupendous primeval volcano existing in the world. The walls up to which we looked are the rim of an irregular circumference of forty miles, averaging 800 feet in height, and enclosing a plain of unsurpassed fertility, embracing over a hundred agricultural villages. The present active peak is within the outer enclosing rim, on the further side from that by which we ascended. As we neared the opening in the enclosing ridge, we could see how, in some inconceivably distant geological epoch, the contents of that mighty cauldron have burst through this fissure, and spread their molten torrents over the vast plain below, to form in after ages by their decomposition the rich black soil of the plains of Higo.

It is a delicious climb, rough though it be under foot; every road, lane, and path is now an avenue of the lovely wax-tree, *Rhus succedanea*, a beautiful, though not a lofty, tree, with wide-spreading branches, and foliage in form and hue something between the ash and the walnut, and in autumn turning to the most exquisite red. From its berries is extracted vegetable wax, one of the most important products of Japan. It has exactly the perfume and appearance of beeswax, and makes very clean candles. Until the introduction of mineral oils from America, and more recently of the electric light, the country was entirely dependent on the illuminating power of the produce of the wax-tree.

I cannot describe the charm of the mountain path as we approached the crest. Waterfalls peeping amongst trees shooting out of cliffs; deep glens below us; festoons of wistaria bloom, painting with purple lines the fresh green foliage of the maples and other nameless trees overhead; a new outline; a new abyss revealed at every turn, till variety itself became monotonous.

We climbed to the top of a ridge, and got our first view of the vast primeval crater. The rim is complete except at this point where the Shirakawa (the one drainage of the whole basin) pours out over the bed of the once glowing lava streams. The diameter of this great crater varies from ten to fourteen miles, and the hundred villages boast of 800 farms. Within this, but at the further side, is an inner crater of much later geologic date, rising to an elevation of 4,150 feet, enclosing an irregular plain, which is comparatively barren and waterless, and then at the further side of this is the innermost, modern, and living volcano of Aso San. I have not seen the volcanoes of the Sandwich Islands, which evidently have points of resemblance with this, but it recalled most vividly the phenomena of the Island of Palma in the Canaries, with this difference, that the Caldera of Palma is only one-third its diameter, but five times its depth, being 4,500 feet from the Pico di Muchacio to the bottom of the crater, which is equally celebrated for its extraordinary fertility, and has a gap through which the lava has flowed in such vast quantities

U

as to cause the well-known pear-shaped form of Palma.

From our ridge we rapidly descended by a mountain path into a deep glen, from the bottom of which rises a column of sulphurous steam. Here are large public hot baths, with lodgings and tea-houses, the baths supplied by bamboo pipes from the boiling springs hard by. They are ingeniously constructed against the side of the hill, and are all open to the path, and both sexes of all ages were enjoying their public parboiling in common in perfect nudity. Just in front of us was a lovely view.

Another deep glen, or rather chasm, joined the one we were following, and the cliffs facing us, several hundred feet high, and all but perpendicular, were clad with forest trees, clinging, one hardly can conceive how, to the face of the cliff. The dashing torrents were fringed with all sorts of ferns, conspicuous among them the giant *Woodwardia japonica*, dropping its fronds to the surface of the stream. We were all enchanted, but we had a walk of some hours before us.

After another hour, arriving at a wayside tea-house, the man with the horses and our luggage declared that here we must stop for the night. I should have said before that when we discharged our kurumas, although one man could easily have carried all we had on his back, we engaged a horse, for which we were charged the enormous sum of forty sen, rather less than twenty pence; and this agreed to, he must needs have a second horse and a friend to accompany him, but as these were on a return journey, they need not be paid for. To have rested at this place would have meant to add another day to our journey and dislocate all our plans, but for some time we were much afraid the strike would have been successful. Every argument was used : we ought to have stayed at the hot baths we had passed ; everyone would be tired ; there would be no food at Tarutama, our proposed destination ; the distance yet to go was, according to their account, greater than when we had started in the morning ; and finally, as a clinching argument, there would be no policemen there to look at our passports ! At last the men were heard to say, 'There is no help for it. If we don't go on, things won't do,' and on we went. Oh, such shrubs ! Wistaria, deutzia, wiegelia, daphne of three or four sorts, wild roses of three species, honeysuckles of two, azaleas of all sorts, a shrub that looked like a white fuchsia, which I never saw before or since, and many others quite strange to us all.

After a long climb we halted in a sort of Devonshire lane for afternoon tea and a rest, the ladies having brought all paraphernalia for tea-making, and a little rill supplying the water. More climbing, till about 6 P.M. we were brought up short by our narrowing valley becoming a gorge, and finally a *cul-de-sac* with a cliff some hundreds of feet high in front, covered with wood, and a cascade of hot water dashing down it. We had arrived at

Tarutama. Under the cliff a long row of two-storied sheds crammed with people, a sort of square in front, two sides of which were formed by large open baths under roofs, but with no enclosing walls, fed by bamboo pipes, with the hot sulphurous water from the foot of the cascade providing a continuous stream through the fully tenanted baths. The place has great renown, especially for rheumatism. There were only two hundred people here now, but as summer approached they expected the number to rise to eight hundred. All the baths are free as well as public, and a great boon to the poor they must be. A very clean native hotel has lately been put up at the entrance to the place, and we soon arranged for supper, bed and breakfast at thirty sen, about a shilling a-piece. Mr. Lang and I had a large room downstairs, and the ladies two rooms upstairs, reached by a ladder from the kitchen. We should have liked a hot bath, but it was hopeless. Our landlord comforted us by telling us that there would not be many bathers in the early hours after midnight. Foreigners were evidently rare visitors here, and we were watched and followed by crowds in our every movement. As our room had no walls, privacy was impossible, but all was exquisitely clean, and the supper of rice and mushroom soup very good.

Next morning I woke at four, a still, starlit night, and pushing the paper frame aside, went across to the nearest bath. There was only one occupant when I arrived, the water was as hot as I could bear it, but

I soon got acclimatized, and enjoyed my swim exceedingly. On my return, I roused Mr. Lang, who followed my example, but had half-a-dozen companions. After a short doze under my futon again, the room was cleared for breakfast. The ladies had succeeded in having an apology for a tub upstairs, a

COUNTRY PEOPLE CARRYING FIREWOOD.

great concession to foreign prejudices. The baggage was all sent down with a man and horse to Tochino-ki, on the other route, where we had arranged before leaving Kumamoto that kurumas were to meet us, and with a guide carrying a lunch basket we started for another steep walk to the summit of Aso San.

Our night's halt had been on the outside of the rim of the middle crater, which is about five miles across. We now soon lost the trees, and were on bare grassy hills until we reached the crest. Then a magnificent panorama of mountain ranges, one encircling the other, was spread before us. No agriculture, only cattle and many horses and foals, and the cuckoo's note resounding all day. Two hours off on our left the rising column of smoke marked Aso San. The path was easy, not steep, and the turf pleasant walking. After four hours we were at the end of vegetation, the last flower being a lovely, pale-blue gentian in great abundance, and we were at the foot of the cone. Here was a little village with tea-houses. Depositing the luncheon basket, we set out for a half-hour's scramble over bare scoria and tufa to the edge of the living crater. It has a double rim; a slight descent from the outer one leads to the very edge of the gulf, on which is perched a tiny shrine of Buddha. It was blowing a gale of wind—fortunately at our backs, otherwise we could not have ascended. I never saw a more wonderful sight than when I looked down that abyss. It is about 950 feet deep, and two-thirds of a mile in circumference. The roar was deafening, and the steam and smoke rose in thick clouds. Fortunately, being to windward, we could see the bottom, and the glowing red-hot tufa and sulphur, as fire and steam seemed to pour forth from the whole surface. Vesuvius and Etna, as I have seen them, are nothing in comparison with the weird Aso San. It is a scene for Doré to have painted.

There is one corner where men can get down to gather the sulphur, and one to whom we spoke had been down the day we were there. Every year some lose their lives in doing so, both by suffocation from the fumes, and from their sinking through the treacherous crust into the molten metal. We did not respond to the invitation to go down, which had to be made by signs, for the roar was too deafening for a word to be heard.

We returned to the tea-house at the base of the cone for luncheon. Our guide utilized the opportunity for setting forth Christianity to a score of attentive listeners. One opponent vehemently urged as an objection that each nation ought to be independent, and that Japan as a great nation should have a god to herself, and not go to foreign gods. One of the ladies had brought a tin of preserved peaches and begged the landlord's acceptance of a plate of them. He lifted the plate to his head in token of acceptance, and then with chopsticks cleverly cut the peaches into small morsels, and going round the crowd, with the chopsticks put a bit into the mouth of each bystander.

We took an entirely different route on our return, in order to visit the geysers of Yunotan. After crossing the rim of the middle crater over grassy downs, and then descending into a lovely valley, wooded in many places, a two hours' walk brought us to a deep gorge, from which arose clouds of smoke, or rather steam. Here was another village of baths, tea-houses, and lodging-sheds. The hot, steaming baths, into which streams were poured by bamboo tubes from the geysers, were as public and as frequented as those we had seen before. Two or three hundred yards above a cluster of geysers poured forth their jets with a deafening roar. The largest sent up a pillar of boiling water and mud to a height of twenty feet. Every few seconds the column seemed to drop two or three feet, and then immediately to rise again. A number of stones of various sizes were shot up with the mud, and often, but not always, dropped outside. Three or four other geysers a little higher up the valley shot up columns quite as large in volume, but only to about half the height. The place seems very little known, and is quite retired from any ordinary thoroughfare, but is very popular as a health resort for the poor. At these baths, as at those we visited on the previous day, the sheds, for they are really nothing better, where the visitors are sheltered at night are maintained by the local authorities, and the lodging as well as the baths are free. They are indeed a great boon to the poor, for rheumatism in all its forms is exceptionally prevalent in Japan, and no wonder, when we see the poor labourers of both sexes working all day knee deep in the mud and water of the paddy fields. We were assured that they rarely fail of effecting a cure, and in the very worst cases give considerable relief. Some patients would sit in the water at a temperature of 100° F. for six hours at a time. The water must be very strongly impregnated with sulphur, as it forms a deep incrustation all round the geysers. Thence we had a very long trudge through a lovely wooded valley to Tochinoki, where the road commences, and we were to find our kurumas. The warm spring weather had evoked abundant insect life, and I added, in these two days, many choice specimens of butterflies to my collection. We were again in the breach through which the lava in old geologic time had broken through the crater, a little to the north of the path by which we had entered, and we looked through it on to the vast plain stretching down to the sea, with Kumamoto at its further end. The sun had set, and it was near eight P.M. when, refreshed by tea, we started for our seventeen miles' ride to the city. Bravely did the tough little kuruma men trot along, and with only one halt to allow them to eat their rice and rest a little, we reached our hospitable friends' house at twenty minutes before midnight.

The next day we turned our faces north again, having each a kuruma with two men, for we had sixteen miles, nearly all uphill, before we should reach the railway terminus to catch the train. When some five miles from our destination the tyre came off one of my wheels. The mishap could not be repaired on the spot, and we could only push on on foot as quickly as possible to the next village, our baggage being on the remaining kuruma. Happily there is no difficulty in finding vehicles even in the most out-of-the-way places, and we reached the terminus in time.

We left the train again at Kurume, our object being to visit the interesting Christian village of

Oyamada. Kurume, though a town of 35,000 inhabitants, seems to consist of one endless street, running up towards the hills; but at last, like Harley Street, it came to an end, and at a tea-house on the edge of the country we enjoyed a delicious native dinner of shrimps, a kind of whitebait, mushroom soup, eggs, and rice. I felt quite satisfied with my management of chopsticks, when the crowd of boys who were watching us did not see anything to laugh at.

Thence we ran along the banks of a river, fringed with ferns and shaded by wax-trees, till we reached an avenue at Korasan, where is a fine Shinto temple on the wooded hill, with a grand view. We had sent our wheels round to meet us at the base of the hill on the other side. At a tea-house in the temple grounds we saw the whole process of preparing green tea for home consumption. The leaves, brought in in large baskets, are steamed in a perforated pan over a boiler on a charcoal fire. They are then spread out on bamboo mats in the sun to dry, but before they become crisp are roughly rolled in the palms of the hand by women. Then the drying is completed, and the leaves are ready for use. We were told that to make black tea for foreign use they bake the leaves after steaming. We drank some delicious fresh tea made from leaves which were on the bushes only a few days ago.

Here our friend Mr. Hutchinson, from Fukuoka, met us, and at the foot of the hill we took ourselves to our kurumas, and were off for Oyamada.

We had a long two hours' ride, shaded by wax-trees as we skirted the range, when, in a village embosomed in trees, we suddenly turned up a steep hill in the narrowest of lanes, under deep shade. At an opening among the trees we got out, and in front of us was a pretty wooden church, with its solid roof and neat porch, in an enclosure ornamented after the fashion of the country with large boulders, brought and arranged with no slight labour : and by its side a picturesque little parsonage of two stories, standing in its garden, very like a Swiss châlet. The church, which will hold three hundred, is tastefully furnished, and, like the parsonage, was built by the people themselves. The catechist, whose wife had been for ten years a pupil of Mrs. Goodall, a benevolent missionary at Nagasaki, and speaks English well, entertained us with tea and cakes. We then climbed by a narrow path to the house of the chief man of the village and the first Christian. Near his house was a natural platform, a little grassy knoll projecting from the hill-side, where the people often assemble to sing hymns. From this spot we had a striking view of the slopes and the village below. Every house is isolated, and the brown roofs peer here and there amongst a dense mass of foliage, the flat tops of the wax-trees.

The story of this village is very interesting. Four years before my visit there was not a Christian in the place; we were here in the centre of Xavier's labours. It is marvellous how, in spite of persecution and isolation, a tradition of Christianity had remained.

In some of the villages the people had preserved a few leaves of old missals, some crosses and other Christian relics. These were kept buried in boxes under the floor in the centre room of a house, and once a year at dead of night, after the house had been carefully shut up, the relics were opened and shown, the sign of the cross made, and the children told it was the proscribed religion of their ancestors. But they knew nothing more. When the country was opened, and religion proclaimed free, some of these villages declared themselves Christian, and at once received the Roman missionaries.

The people of Oyamada noticed that the conduct and life of the inhabitants of one of these villages was far superior to that of the Buddhists, and came to the conclusion that it must be a good religion which produced such fruits. Some of them went to the government office at the neighbouring town of Kurume, and talked to the officials there of their intention of inquiring into Christianity. They replied to them: 'If you want to be Christians, do not go to the old Christians, for they brought all the trouble to Japan many years ago by meddling in politics; go to the new Christians, for they never interfere with Japanese matters of state.' They were also told that if they went to Nagasaki, they would hear all about Christianity; so a deputation set out along with the head of the village on what was to them a very serious journey. Arrived at Nagasaki, they went to an inn, but the people there knew nothing about any Christians, when a bystander said: 'I know all the foreigners, and will take you to them. But you don't know their ways; you can do nothing with them unless you give them a dinner first. Give me $30, and I will provide the dinner, and make all right.' But they cautiously replied that they would wait and see the foreigners first. The man took them to the Church Missionary Society bookshop, and it turned out that all he knew of the matter was the existence of this shop. The colporteur sent them to Mr. Hutchinson, and they began by producing, in true Japanese fashion from handkerchiefs, two large tins of mutton, which they had brought as an introductory present. Mr. Hutchinson heard their story, felt satisfied of their sincerity, and told them he would send them two teachers to instruct them in the religion of Jesus, but they must expect no money nor any worldly advantage. He sent Mr. Nakamura, the present catechist, and another.

Some months afterwards he was summoned to examine their catechumens. He baptized seventy at the house of the head man whom we visited, and soon after twenty more whom he had put back for further instruction. There were now 140 well-instructed Christians there. Bishop Bickersteth afterwards visited them for confirmation; and one man, who was not able to be present, afterwards walked fifty miles to receive the rite at Fukuoka. They maintain a Christian school. Formerly near the spot where the church has been built were two trees which were considered sacred, and between them hung the sacred straw rope connected with Shinto worship. When two-thirds of the villagers had become Christians, the sons of the head man boldly cut down the sacred trees in the middle of the night, and they have been used to form the roof-tree of the church, while a sacred stone with an inscription has been inverted and made the threshold of the church.

The village was not without its troubles. The Japanese are extremely fond of lawsuits, and it is commonly said that each village considers it an honourable distinction to have been involved in a suit with her neighbours. Oyamada has been no exception. There was a bit of common land claimed both by it and by a neighbouring village. Their old maps differed from those of their neighbours, and both were of great antiquity. They had had a lawsuit for some years about it, which was carried through four courts, till at last, in the High Court of Tokio, they lost it. The bit of land was worth about $1000, and the costs they had to pay came to $8000, so Chancery suits and law expenses exist elsewhere than in England. Reluctantly we bid good-bye to Oyamada, and went down the hill to our kurumas.

In passing through Kurume I noticed the shop of a knife-handle manufacturer. He had an immense stock of horns and skins of the deer of the country (*Cervus sika*), which he told me was very common, of which I secured specimens. He informed me that there was another deer to be found in Kiushiu, much rarer, but of which he had at present no specimens. After an unsuccessful hunt after bronzes and lacquer, we resumed our journey by train, and reached Fukuoka before midnight, glad of a few days' rest, which I spent in entomological researches in the woods, and antiquarian in the city.

I had an invitation to visit the collection of a Japanese doctor, who had a reputation as an entomologist. When we called, he had gone on a professional visit into the country, but we were told by the servant that the lady of the house would be glad to see us. She, a sweet aristocratic-looking Japanese lady, had the keys of her husband's cabinets, and kindly allowed me to examine everything at leisure. I derived much information from my visit on the marked differences between the lepidoptera of Kiushiu and those of the main island, a very large proportion being representative species. Then the lady insisted on showing us her collection of old Satsuma china, which she evidently held much more deserving of notice than her husband's insects, and it really was such a collection as could not now be brought together unless at considerable expenditure.

I was afterwards fortunate enough to obtain in Fukuoka, in a second-hand shop in the lower part of the town, the only two specimens of old Satsuma crackled ware that I met with for sale. Here, too, as we were out of the beat of ordinary tourists, I secured several specimens of antique bronzes. These things, though easily obtained at the first opening of the country, often now fetch higher prices in Japan than in Europe. Whilst ransacking the old curiosity shops in company with my kind friend and host Mr. Hind, as we left one shop in which we were attended to by the mistress only, her husband being out, Mr. Hind asked me if I had not been struck by her appearance. I said I noticed that she had not only a handsome, but a remarkably long and oval face. He replied that she had all the marks of the most aristocratic Japanese type, and he was determined to find out who she was. Upon inquiry it was ascertained that she was the daughter of a Daimio of high rank, who had been ruined in the Satsuma rebellion.

From Fukuoka my face was turned homeward, or rather further from home, across the Pacific to Vancouver. We retraced our steps to Mōji, and crossed the famous Straits of Shimanoseki to Bakan, the town on main island side, where we rested a night waiting for the steamer; then through the Inland Sea, of which the traveller can never tire, though the reader may; a few days at Osaka; a halt at Kioto, and then at Tokio for farewell visits; and I am once more embarked on a Canadian Pacific boat, and reluctantly bid farewell to the enchanting Land of the Rising Sun as we steer towards Columbia's western shore.

INDEX.

Arima, 30.
Armour, 57, 58.
Aso San, volcano of, 291-295.
Austin, Rev. W. T., work of, 34.
Awaji, Island of, 247, 261.

Bathing arrangements, 147, 197.
Birds, 63, 64, 105, 106, 120, 121, 122.
Biwa, Lake of, 187.
Bridges, 84, 85, 86, 258.
Buddha, images of, 105, 141, 204.
    sacred horse of, 98.

Cherry-trees, 35, 50.
Chinese language, uses of, 114.
Christian educators, 39, 208, 237, 238.
    relics, 46.
Chusenji, Lake of, 107-113.
Climate, 19, 20.
Cloisonné ware, 175, 177.
Coal mining, 22, 23, 268, 269.
Cormorant fishing, 181.
Cryptomerias, 83, 108, 116.
Czarevitch, assault upon, 188, 190.

Dazaifu, 277.
Deshima, 13, 15.
Doshisha, 208.

Earthquake, 73.
Emperor's gardens, Kioto, 211, 212.
    palaces, 41, 219.
"English as she is spoke," 136, 137, 197.
English language, spread of, 114.

Falconry, 94, 97, 98.
Fisheries, 21, 258, 261.
Fishing-tackle, 62.
Flower show at Osaka, 245.
Formosa, Island of, 20.
Fruit-trees, 35.
Fuji San, mountain of, 127.
    origin of word, 162.

Fukuoka, 269-276.

Geysers of Yunotan, 295.
Gifu, 180, 182.
Gotemba, 153.

Hakone, 138, 142.
Hawking, 94, 97, 98.
Heraldry, 40.
Hideyoshi, 226, 227.
Hieizan, mountain of, 214, 215.
Hikone, 184, 187.
Hotels, 86, 87, 88, 90, 112, 153, 155, 184, 192.

Inland sea, 24, 25, 266, 267, 268.
Insignia, 39, 40.
Iyeyasu, 91, 92.
    temples and mausoleum of, 90, 93, 98-101.
Irrigation, 144, 287.

Japanese courtesy, 163.
    eating customs, 155, 156.
    literalness, 153, 154.
    love of the beautiful, 14, 15, 109.
    sponge-cake, 88.
Jinrikshas, 35, 42.

Kammon-ga-fuchi, 102.
Karasaki, pine-trees near, 189.
Kiushiu, Island of, 19, 266-285.
Kioto, 195-222.
    industrial exhibition, 213.
Kobe, 24.
Kozu, 128.
Kumamoto, 279, 280, 283.

Lamps, bronze and stone, 50.

Match factory in Osaka, 241.
Mausoleums, 100, 271, 284.
May day, 71.

Minerals, 21, 22.
Missions at Gifu, 182.
        Fukuoko, 269, 272-275.
        Kumamoto, 280.
        Kurume, 300, 301, 302.
        Nagasaki, 16.
        Osaka, 229-234.
        Shikoku, 247.
        Tokio, 73, 74.
        Tokushima, 250-256.
Miya-no-Shita, journey to, 133, 134.
Museums, 45, 46, 47.
    Nagasaki, 13, 15, 16.
    Nagoya, 165-180.
    Naruto, 261, 262.
Neeshima, Joseph, 208, 211, 212.
Nijo, castle of, 221, 222.
Nikko, 81-123.
      cascades near, 106, 109, 119.
      journey to, 81, 82, 83, 84.
Nippon, Island of, 19.

Odawara, 128, 129.
Osaka, 30, 225-246.
Otsu, 189, 190.

Parliament-house, 41.
Passports, 81.
Painting, 177.
Pheasants, 89.
      feathers exported, 89.
Poaching, 107.
Porcelain, making of, 175, 176, 177.
      packing of, 178.

Railway station luncheons, 165.
      travelling, 35, 81, 128, 164, 172, 184, 268, 269, 279.
Ronins, legend of, 66, 69.

Sailors' home, 34.

Satsuma ware, 175, 176.
Schools, 39, 53, 208, 230, 237, 238.
Shiba, 57, 70.
Shikoku, Island of, 247-265.
      voyage to, 248.
Shinto temples, 47, 48, 111.
Shodo Shonin, legends of, 85, 86.
Shoguns, 40, 65.
      shrines of, 50, 65.
St. Andrew's school, 76.
St. Hilda's school, 77.
Straw bridges, 110.
     sandals, 110.
Sulphur baths, 141, 148, 292, 296.

Taxidermists' shops, 62.
Tarutama, 292.
Tea drinking, 242.
    making, 298.
Temples, 47, 66, 90-102, 161, 170, 171, 172, 191, 198-208, 218, 229, 253, 277, 278.
Tides at Naruto, 262.
Tokio, 35, 36.
    university of, 53.
Tokushima, 250-257.
Trees, dwarfing and transplanting, 54.
    preservation of, 269.
Tycoon, meaning of, 40.

Uyeno, 42, 45, 46.

Volcano of Aso San, 291-295.

Water travelling, 24, 248, 249, 250, 266, 267.
Wax-trees, 288.
Women, clothing of, 23.

Yezzo, island of, 19.
Yokohama, 33.

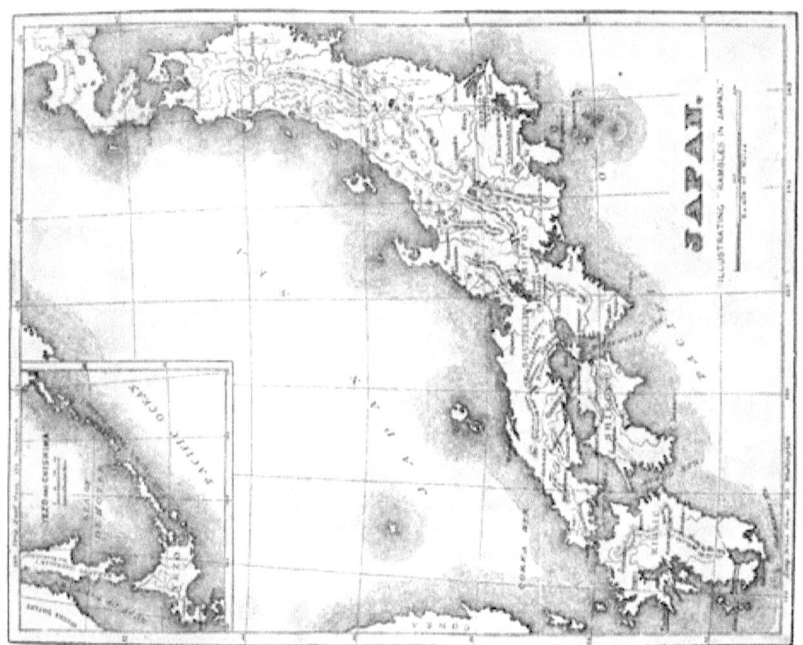

www.ingramcontent.com/pod-product-compliance
Lightning Source LLC
Chambersburg PA
CBHW022104230426
43672CB00008B/1275